Embodied Approaches to Supervision

T0373570

Embodied Approaches to Supervision presents innovative approaches to working with the body in supervision.

The authors, who are all experts in their field, bring a wealth of experience and knowledge to each chapter, raising the reader's awareness of the value of working with the body in the supervisory relationship. With the help of case vignettes, the book offers reflections on the intimate and dynamic interaction between mind and body and how to work with this in supervision. It presents diverse approaches to practice, where the body is at the centre of facilitating reflection and containment of supervisees, either in one-to-one or group contexts, in person and online. Readers gain insight about how embodiment is attended to within as well as outside of the session in the context of self-supervision.

This text will be of value to supervisors and supervisors-in-training, practitioners seeking supervision and anyone keen to learn more about embodied approaches in supervision.

Céline Butté, MA, is a UKCP and ADMP registered dance movement psychotherapist, a supervisor and one of the core teachers on the Creative Supervision Diploma with the London Centre for Psychodrama. She co-edited *Dance Movement Psychotherapy with People with Learning Disabilities: Out of the Shadows, into the Light* (2017) and has authored several other publications.

Tasha Colbert, PG (dip), is a UKCP and ADMP registered dance movement psychotherapist, supervisor and co-director of The Institute of Embodied Psychotherapy where she is a trainer on the Certificate in Integrative Embodied Psychotherapy. She has also co-edited the book *Working across Modalities in the Arts Therapies: Creative Collaborations*, Routledge (2017).

"Many psychotherapists today realise the importance of attending to non-verbal embodied communications in psychotherapy. However, supervision still tends to rely on the verbal exchange; the supervisee presents a case, and the supervisor provides comments verbally.

Many years of experience with embodied approaches to supervision have convinced me that supervisees hold important unconscious knowledge about themselves and their patients in their bodies. I believe it is the supervisor's responsibility to help the supervisee to gain access to her/his own experience.

In this volume on embodied approaches to supervision, Céline Butté and Tasha Colbert have collected several innovative ways to engage the body in the supervision process. I therefore highly recommend this book to those who wish to learn how body-based approaches enhance psychotherapy supervision."

Jon Sletvold, *Author of* The Embodied Analyst –
From Freud and Reich to Relationality

"The hybrid nature of this book reflects the increased interest in cross-modalities in supervision. It presents diverse approaches with the body as the site of reflection and containment illustrated by case vignettes. This rich collection of inspiring chapters makes a very valuable contribution to all psychotherapists and counsellors who wish to learn more about creative embodied approaches in supervision."

Helen Payne, *Professor, PhD, Reg. ADMP UK & UKCP,
Chair in Psychotherapy, University of Hertfordshire, UK, Author in,
and Editor of*, Essentials of Dance Movement Psychotherapy:
International Perspectives from Theory, Research and Practice

"A valuable addition to the literature which rightfully gives prominence to the body, and shows that it is possible to work somatically online."

Robin and Joan Shohet, *Co-authors of* In Love with Supervision

"The creativity of the authors contributing to this book is based on rich and profound knowledge; their wealth of ideas, theoretical and practical, is remarkable. Their focus is clear: the embodied care in the supervisory context. My experience of reading this book is of being moved, touched and inspired as well as feeling a resonance with my own thinking and practice."

Hilda Wengrower, *DMT, PhD, Co-editor of* Dance and Creativity
within Dance Movement Therapy: International Perspectives

Embodied Approaches to Supervision

The Listening Body

Edited by Céline Butté and
Tasha Colbert

LONDON AND NEW YORK

Cover image: © Getty Images

First published 2023
by Routledge
4 Park Square, Milton Park, Abingdon, Oxon OX14 4RN

and by Routledge
605 Third Avenue, New York, NY 10158

Routledge is an imprint of the Taylor & Francis Group, an informa business

© 2023 selection and editorial matter, Céline Butté & Tasha Colbert; individual chapters, the contributors

British Library Cataloguing-in-Publication Data
A catalogue record for this book is available from the British Library

ISBN: 9780367473358 (hbk)
ISBN: 9780367473341 (pbk)
ISBN: 9781003034940 (ebk)

DOI: 10.4324/9781003034940

Typeset in Times New Roman
by Newgen Publishing UK

Contents

Figures

Contributors

Céline Butté, MA, ADMP UK, UKCP, is a dance movement psychotherapist, a supervisor and one of the core teachers on the Creative Supervision Diploma with the London Centre for Psychodrama. She co-edited *Dance Movement Psychotherapy with People with Learning Disabilities: Out of the Shadows, into the Light* (2017) and authored other publications dedicated to creative embodied approaches to psychotherapy and supervision.

Roz Carroll, MA, UKCP, is a relational body psychotherapist, a supervisor and a trainer. She taught the M.A. in Integrative Psychotherapy at The Minster Centre for 14 years. She is the co-editor, with Jane Ryan, of *What is Normal? Psychotherapists Explore the Question* (Confer 2020) and an author of numerous articles and chapters.

Anna Chesner, MA, UKCP registered psychodrama and group analytic psychotherapist and supervisor, is the co-director of the London Centre for Psychodrama Group and Individual Psychotherapy and founder-director of its cross-professional Creative Supervision Diploma course. She has worked as a psychotherapist within the NHS and prison service and currently offers psychotherapy and supervision in private practice in London. Anna is widely published in the field of action methods.

Sue Curtis, BA Ed, MA, ADMP UK, lectures and supervises Goldsmiths, University of London's DMP training and guest-lectured in Barcelona, Ukraine, Poland, Latvia and Germany. She also engages in the work of ADMP UK. Sue has published on themes of death and bereavement, the sensory landscape and the notion of hope when living with serious illness. She supervises privately incorporating creative modalities.

Katy Dymoke, BMCA, ADMP UK, PCU, Body Psychotherapy Network, is a dance movement psychotherapist and a supervisor. Whilst as an NHS employee, she undertook sponsored doctoral research into the impact of touch on her practice, now completing a PhD by publication. Teacher and Program Director of the Body-Mind Centering® practitioner programme, with Embody-Move, she specialises in dance for visually impaired people with Touchdown Dance.

Yeva Feldman, ADMP UK, UKCP, is a registered Gestalt movement psychotherapist and supervisor. She co-convenes the MA DMP programme at the University of Roehampton and teaches in the UK and abroad. Her publications include research and practice with individuals living with eating disorders and an embodied approach to working with trauma.

Martin Gill, MSc UKCP, HCPC, BPA, BADth, is a dramatherapist, psychodramatist, supervisor and a trained couple therapist in private practice. He has been delivering training on supervision and action methods for many years to a range of organisations including the International Family Therapy Association and the UK Association of Family Therapy.

Christina Greenland, ADMP UK, HCPC (OT), is an occupational therapist and a dance movement psychotherapist. She has worked across community and inpatient mental health settings within the NHS since 2008. Christina has also managed various NHS services, including a Gender Identity Clinic, where she deepened her understanding of body, gender and identity.

Bryn Jones, MA, BaDTh, HCPC, is a dramatherapist and a clinical supervisor. He is a lecturer on the Drama and Movement Therapy MA at Royal Central School University of London and a member of the teaching team on the *Creative Approaches to Supervision* Postgraduate Diploma with the London Centre for Psychodrama. His current supervisory practice includes individual supervision for MA-level students and therapists from a broad range of modalities.

Julie Joseph, ADMP UK, APSE, is a Director of Common Thread, a Scottish company offering therapeutic residential care and education to vulnerable young people. She has worked with adolescents for over 15 years and as a movement psychotherapist within the care and education sector.

Therese O'Driscoll, SIAHIP, EAP, MASP, is a psychotherapist, a supervisor and a movement practitioner. She works from her wild garden and cabin studio in the North West of Ireland called An Talamh, meaning ground of the earth, emphasising embodied, embedded and emergent practices (see thereseodriscoll.ie for further details).

Annette Schwalbe, MA, MSC, DMP UK, UKCP, is a dance movement psychotherapist, a supervisor and a somatic body mapping practitioner. She is a counselling co-ordinator at Kinergy, a specialist service for survivors of sexual abuse and violence. Her work is informed by feminist theory and creative, body-led practice.

www.annetteschwalbe.co.uk & mail@annetteschwalbe.co.uk

Hannah Sherbersky, DClinPrac, UKCP, AFT (Association of Family Therapy), is a systemic family and couples psychotherapist and supervisor. As the deputy director of CEDAR at the University of Exeter, she is also interested in the innovative delivery of creative and integrative ideas, recently contributing to a BBC3 family therapy documentary, various podcasts and an online app.

All contributing authors are based in the UK.

Foreword

This anthology is a welcome addition to a growing body of literature that supports embodied approaches to supervision. It is heartening to witness how this community of experienced practitioners brings moving bodies unapologetically into a central focus. The chapters are cradled within an atmosphere of creativity and multiplicity, in which supervisors navigate the specificities of their discipline, whilst the anthology-as-a-whole moves in and out, across and through methods, paradigms and practices. As a collection, this work evidences some of the many ways to practice embodied supervision and, as I read, I am inspired to reflect on my own work as both supervisor and supervisee with individuals and groups, across indoor, outdoor and online settings. At the same time, I am reminded of the importance of holding my beliefs in the efficacy of any one paradigm lightly. Reading this anthology reminds me how paradigms, methods, approaches and techniques are useful containers, as they sharpen my focus. Yet, I am mindful that paradigms, methods, approaches and techniques in themselves are abstract notions without the ethical integrity and deep experience of the delivering practitioner. Regardless of the perspective from which we practice, what is crucial to the process of supervising is the kind of thinking that we bring and the kind of knowledge-ing that underpins that practice, to ensure that the method itself does not obscure what it is that needs to be revealed. Perhaps when we are new to engaging in the role of supervisor, we might rely more heavily on techniques and structures. Experience brings increasing confidence in our capacity to be flexible and responsive in the moment, whilst retaining an embodied ethical intent that is focused on the task in hand. As we develop our practice of supervision, we become increasingly skilled at holding contradictions and creating pathways through liminal spaces, thus creating worlds within worlds in which boundaries become ethical, permeable and fluid. This listening supervisor's body of mine needs to be vigilant, remaining alert to less-conscious biases that determine how I privilege knowledge in my practice. When I catch myself becoming too sure of my own knowing as a supervisor, the world usually sends me a challenge that disrupts any complacency that might be setting in.

As a supervisor, I am tasked with an ethical (a commitment to working responsibly with power relations), material (an affective, embodied, relational presence) and discursive (an engagement with discourses that shape our conceptualisations) commitment to bringing to light insights into the Supervisees' professional practice. The chapters in this anthology illustrate how ethical, material-discursive commitments can manifest in different ways; the common denominator being the way in which the listening body is activated in embodied supervision. Supervisors can foster this listening body through sensed, felt, intuitive experience as well as spontaneous improvisation. Sometimes knowledge manifests in a momentary glance, a breath, a silence, a shift of the body or a sigh. This is the thinking body at work, which moves beyond representational language as it responds to tender, embryonic moments of not-yet-formed insights emerging into fruition. At the same time, we have a duty as supervisors to engage with critical theory, as we commit to developing anti-oppressive language and practice that challenges historical oppressions that are infused into the intersections of individual subjectivities. These include, for example, issues of gender, sexual identity, race, ethnicity, disability, class religion, spiritual beliefs, age and anthropocentrism. These intersections are collective concerns and, during supervision, we are inside the currents of their micro, mezzo and macro entangled manifestations.

Time was, supervisors grew into their role through clinical experience, rather than through formal supervision training. For example, in earlier days, Dance Movement Psychotherapy (DMP) practitioners who were registered with the Association for DMP UK (ADMP UK) became supervisors through a registration route, requiring them to demonstrate sufficient discipline-specific, supervised clinical postgraduation experience to apply to be a senior registered practitioner and join the supervisor's register. Like many others in the field, I followed this pathway to becoming a clinical supervisor and after supervising for some time, I decided to further consolidate my skills by enrolling in a Diploma in Supervision at the Society for Analytical Psychology (SAP). At that time, I was the only DMP amongst verbal psychotherapists and Jungian analysts and found myself needing to stand my ground in relation to privileging embodied ways of knowing as at least equal to language and discourse. At times, I was surprised to be confronted by my own tendency to subordinate the material, moving body in relation to language and discursive practice, realising that, despite my rhetoric, this cultural phenomenon of the dominance of language and discourse was deeply inscribed in me.

Since that time, the language of embodiment has found its way into mainstream psychotherapy practice and the chapters in this book are a testament to the pioneering work of supervisors who, over the decades, have enlivened embodied dwelling places inherent in the supervisory process. The authors illustrate how the thinking body carries imagination, play and incisive analysis and the writing styles straddle the prosaic and the poetic, with critical analysis woven skilfully into practice-led thinking. This diversity of styles reflects the mercurial experience of animating the listening body in supervision.

This work has come into being through a pandemic and as such records how embodied practitioners have embraced online practice, navigating this techno-mediated space of connectivity. The authors articulate how the pandemic brought working online, which was previously more of an exception, as a new normativity.

Regulatory bodies were prompted to update and develop ethical guidelines for supervising online and this anthology references adaptations and opportunities for working through a screen. For example, in face-to-face supervision indoors, the supervisor usually takes responsibility for the physical environment and in outdoor supervision, both supervisor and supervisee navigate a shared outdoor space together. However, in online supervision, supervisor and supervisee are connected in time, but not in space and this anthology addresses the ethical, as well as the practical challenges and opportunities that this presents.

The diversity of perspectives offered by these authors, including the potential for online working, honours the many ways that the listening body can create a safe contained space in which to explore the waters of the clinical work. The content reminds me that as a supervisor I can move in, from and to many directions, holding a multiplicity of possibilities, as well as remaining in touch with the humility of my own limitations. This book helps me to dare to move simultaneously into and away from what I think I know. As I immerse myself in the immediacy of any particular moment as a supervisor, I never quite know what will arrive. In that moment of responding, I reach into the well of knowledge, as I struggle to tune into my listening body and fumble for an at least good enough intervention. In that fraction of a second, I listen to my intuition, my heart and my emotions. I notice the sensations that course through my body. I allow methodologies, approaches, discourses and analyses to brush through my thoughts. I identify and disidentify with stories, imaginings and experiences of my own. My ego changes gear and then does so again. And in that (sometimes fraction of a) second, I have a choice in making the next move that will affect the direction(s) of this supervisory inquiry. As it might be said that each client brings a uniqueness that requires a unique approach, so each supervisee will need particular responsiveness from their supervisor. This anthology of works serves as a reminder of the many vertices from which I can engage with the delicate task of supervision. There is not just one way; however, there is always an ethical obligation to remain in touch with the good enough threads of my material-discursive professional practice, as I immerse myself in the waves of the supervisory inquiry. I trust that you will enjoy as much as I have, an immersion in the supervisory waters of the content of this anthology.

Caroline Frizell

Caroline Frizell, PhD, UKCP, ADMP, Dip Sup SAP is a senior lecturer on the MA Dance Movement Psychotherapy at Goldsmiths University and convened the programme for a decade. Caroline is committed to posthuman, eco-feminist research and practice in psychotherapy and supervision indoors, outdoors and online. She has extensive publications that intersect DMP, ecopsychotherapy, supervision and critical disability studies.

Introduction

Céline Butté and Tasha Colbert

Movement and the body are an essential aspect of supervision, whether we explicitly work with the body or not. The interest of this book is in the intentional focus on the body and movement and how this can serve the supervisory process. The question of how to reach that fertile ground where supervisor and supervisee feel safe enough to tap into the wisdom of the body is explored in depth.

Embodied Approaches to Supervision: The Listening Body presents innovative approaches and reflective accounts of working with the body in supervision. The supervisory interventions presented in each chapter open up new ways of seeing, listening and understanding through embodied processes. The authors, all experts in their fields, each bring a wealth of experience and knowledge, raising our awareness of the value of working with the body in the supervisory relationship. The hybrid nature of the book reflects the current climate of cross-modality fertility in the world of psychotherapy and supervision practice at large and comes as only the latest in a lineage of publications dedicated to articulating our understanding of embodied processes in supervision, including 'Supervision in Dance Movement Therapy' (Payne, 2008); various publications on supervision by dance movement psychotherapists (Panhofer, Payne, Meekums, & Parke, 2011; Frizell, 2012); 'Creative Supervision across Modalities' (Chesner & Zografou, 2014) and 'Working with Embodiment in Supervision: A Systemic Approach' (Bownas & Fredman, 2017). Following on from its predecessors, this book offers further insights into how embodiment is defined and can be attended to within supervision sessions. It presents with clarity diverse approaches to supervision practice where the body is at the centre of facilitating the reflection and containment of supervisees, in both a one-to-one and a group context. In addition, each chapter contains case vignettes illustrating the application of a particular supervision model, whether working in person, online, indoors or outside or in the context of self-supervision.

Taking shape in the midst of the Covid-19 pandemic, the book emerges at a time of unprecedented challenges. So, besides reflecting on their specific approach, some contributors offer reflections on the impact of the pandemic

DOI: 10.4324/9781003034940-1

on their practice. Whilst some supervisors were already providing online supervision prior to the pandemic, Covid-19 restrictions compelled all supervisors and psychotherapists to shift their practice online. Such an adaptation has required resourcefulness, resilience and a revisioning of established practice (Carroll, 2021). It has also highlighted, for those new to online working, that facilitating embodied processes and creative exploration in psychotherapy and supervision is possible within a virtual setting.

And yet it feels important to also acknowledge the differences when we relate solely through a screen. The somatic resonance that takes place between two bodies in a room together, for example – and the information this gives us as practitioners, such as transferential and parallel processes – is different from when we relate through an online platform. Our bodies register the absence of the other and are disorientated by it. This, along with latency (online delay), creates an underlying stressor in video communication (Goldhahn, 2021). Furthermore, the restricted visual frame, with its focus on the face and head, can create a tendency towards solely verbal reflection. Standing back from the screen, shifting the position of the device, as well as standing up and moving all help to make the transition to embodied processes. Several contributors reflect on how they have adapted their approach to working online and raise some important factors to consider. So, just as we acknowledge the losses of working online, we learn of the creativity the medium has stimulated in the profession and discover how practitioners have successfully expanded their practice to include it.

The broader context surrounding the book includes the Black Lives Matter movement, the MeToo campaign, the refugee crisis and increased awareness of climate change, critical events that drive us to question what we know and to engage actively with the realities of the twenty-first century. Finding compassion and empathy, as well as tuning in with our own embodied reality, have become essential means of attending to the many conflicting forces at play in the world and within ourselves. This is the territory in which supervision takes place, whether explicitly addressed or brought implicitly into the mix of our reflective task.

As editors, we naturally reached out to professionals whose work we respect from the BAME (Black, Asian and minority ethnic) community. However, the reality of the context – the commitment and activism inherent to the Black Lives Matter movement and the impact of the pandemic – in several cases meant their energies were expended elsewhere. Undeniably, the absence of representation of BAME supervisors in the book also reflects the wider context of the psychotherapy and supervision profession and its white dominance. Whilst work is being done to improve accessibility to the psychotherapy profession for Black, Asian and minority groups, further change still needs to take place for the profession to reflect the diversity of the society it serves (Turner, 2021). Embodiment enables us to feel into the world of 'the other' as well as shine a light on our own prejudices. Thus, as some authors point out, an embodied approach to supervision enables us to sensitively and explicitly address the chasm between cultures and personal blindspots developed from within our own cultural biases.

This book developed through a shared vision of bringing together the wisdom of practitioners we have been inspired by in our growth as psychotherapists and supervisors. We approached colleagues who 'walk their talk' and have embodied ways of knowing and reflecting in their supervision practice. With a growing wealth of literature on working with the body, it felt essential to gather writing that is embedded in the practice of supervision.

At the time of writing, we are learning to live with Covid-19 and dealing with the traumas and losses it has left on its trail. The project has not been immune to the impact of the pandemic. Authors initially keen to contribute have had to turn their attention to their own health or to personal and professional matters that proved more pressing. As well as celebrating the accomplishment that each chapter represents, it feels important to us to acknowledge the unspoken voices in the following pages.

The ten chapters summarised below present a variety of embodied approaches to supervision rooted in a diverse range of practices including body psychotherapy, psychodrama, eco-supervision, dance movement psychotherapy, family therapy and dramatherapy.

Chapter 1, 'Perspective Taking in Supervision', the opening chapter of this book, brings clarity to the psychodramatic techniques of concretisation and working with role in supervision. Anna Chesner illustrates through several vignettes how these embodied processes can offer multiple perspectives as well as the opportunities for awareness and insight these techniques can bring. The author also reflects on the importance of imagination and attending to the body and movement when working with roles online.

In Chapter 2, 'The Dialogical Dance: A Relational Embodied Approach to Supervision', Yeva Feldman presents an embodied and relational approach to supervision, developed over many years of educating and supervising dance movement psychotherapy trainees. Through compelling vignettes, she demonstrates how the use of embodiment, and more specifically movement in supervision, is fundamentally in the service of our clients, increasing embodied empathy as well as strengthening the supervisees' ability to use their body as a resource in their practice.

Chapter 3, 'Multimodal and Liminal Perspectives (MLP); The Role of Liminality in the Dynamic of the Supervisory Relationship', introduces a new supervisory method (MLP), to support insight in the context of the supervisory relationship. Bryn Jones describes the ways in which both projective and embodied processes are incorporated into the method, and how these deliver a richly textured and contextualised understanding of the key themes being explored. The chapter demonstrates how the MLP method offers both supervisee and supervisor an expansive framework where a particular practice issue can be viewed from multiple perspectives.

In Chapter 4, 'Eco-Supervision – Embodied, Embedded, Emergence in Supervision', Therese O'Driscoll invites us to consider the relationship with the environment as part of the supervisory process. The triad relationship between supervisor, supervisee and the environment is brought to life through an illuminating case example where she describes how an embodied dialogue with the natural world can offer a fresh perspective. The chapter is an invitation to both supervisor and supervisee to develop an embodied ecological consciousness in their work and lives.

Hannah Sherbersky and Martin Gill in Chapter 5: 'The "Four Chair Method" – An Integrative Approach to Creative Supervision', describe an action-based relational supervision process, the Four Chair Method, developed from their integrative supervision practice of family therapy, psychodrama and dramatherapy. Through case vignettes, they show us how the Four Chairs is a purposeful and playful method that is informed by role theory and uses aesthetic distance. This approach is both structured and spontaneous.

Julie Joseph, in Chapter 6: 'Mirroring within Supervision', reflects on how transitioning to online practice due to the pandemic awoke curiosity for the role mirroring can play in supervision with trained psychotherapists as well as non-psychotherapeutically trained members of staff. Through a review of the literature on mirroring within verbal approaches to psychotherapy and dance movement psychotherapy, as well as several vignettes, the author illustrates how supervisors may consciously utilise the mirror neuron pathways to hold supervisees in their reflection on clinical issues.

Chapter 7: 'Reflections on Thresholds and Containers in Supervision' is written by Céline Butté who introduces FERN (a Framework for the Embodied Reflective Narrative), a tool and methodology for working with improvised movement and dance in supervision. Through this chapter, the author draws our attention to principles fundamental to creating safety when stepping in and out of creative embodied processes within supervision. Vignettes illustrate how dwelling in movement improvisation and somatic modes of reflection requires responsibility by the supervisor to be mindful of the thresholds they support their supervisees to cross. The author eloquently describes how attending to 'what gets opened' and 'what gets closed' contains the embodied reflective process.

Roz Carroll, in Chapter 8: 'Supervision beyond Supervision: Widening and Nourishing Embodied Reflexivity as Part of Self-Supervision', reminds us that we are all bodies and therefore embodied, with implications beyond the dedicated focus of a supervision session. The author demonstrates how the act of self-supervision is a reflexive inquiry that takes us beyond the reflective work done with colleagues and outlines the recuperative benefits of transitional activities embedded in daily life. In these multi-sensory contexts, the therapist can move and be immersed in an environment where thoughts, feelings and images flow freely. Evocative vignettes shed light on some of the many facets of embodied reflexivity.

Chapter 9: 'Holding Sacred: The Woman's Body in Supervision', co-authored by Annette Schwalbe, Sue Curtis and Christina Greenland, presents the voices of three women co-authors who speak to their own and each other's bodies in their supervision encounters over time and their multi-faceted supervisory relationships over time. The authors identify key aspects of their supervision experience that hold sacred their embodied presence as woman practitioners in service of their clients. Somatic Body Mapping, developed by Annette Schwalbe, is the creative method used to contain their exploration of the sacred feminine.

In the book's final chapter, Chapter 10: 'Supervision or Co-vision? Co-activating a Receptive and Responsive Container for Reflection and Restoration', Katy Dymoke presents how Body Mind Centering offers a helpful perspective on the relational field in supervision. Drawing on clear embodied anatomical principles, the author invites us to view the supervisory relationship as a co-created phenomenon between supervisor and supervisee and consider the membrane as a useful metaphor in our understanding of supervisory processes.

This book is being published at a time when it has become widely accepted that to work effectively with trauma in psychotherapy, practitioners need to have a knowledge of the body and be able to integrate embodied processes into their practice. When working with the body makes so much sense in psychotherapy, inviting the body to take centre stage in supervision further supports embodied knowledge and integrated practice. As embodied supervisors, we have experienced for ourselves in our own supervision and witnessed in our supervisees, how creative and embodied processes have a restorative function for practitioners, which helps to maintain wellbeing and foster resilience.

Embodied supervision is a holistic endeavour. In their work together, supervisor and supervisee(s) harness various qualities of presence and awareness that include attention to their physiological experience; the possibility of moving in the supervision space; as well as opportunities to interact with the environment. These broadly contrasting qualities of attention nurture the supervisory process and remind us, as Shohet and Shohet state in their latest publication, that 'everything is data' (2021: 21) or as Frizell describes it: 'all matter matters' (2019: lecture).

An embodied approach, such as that described in these pages, lends itself to taking a paradoxical 'both/and', rather than a dualistic 'either/or' approach (Best, 2008: 141; Shohet & Shohet, 2021: 20). As we learn to pay attention to the more uncomfortable 'shadowy' parts of our inner and outer landscape – which can be said to be both a part of us and something we are party to – we move away from the 'othering' that Turner articulates so well (2021: 8). As he explains, 'One of the most powerful starting points for understanding internalised experiences is by working with the body' (ibid: 12). Thus, through a truly embodied practice, our capacity to tolerate and accommodate is increased, and we gain ever greater levels of understanding – to the ultimate benefit of all our clients.

It has been enriching for us to draw together the different voices presented in these pages and to contribute to the field of embodiment in supervision. We hope that *Embodied Approaches to Supervision: The Listening Body* is of value to supervisors, supervisors-in-training and anyone interested in learning more about embodied approaches in supervision.

References

Best, P. (2008). Interactive reflections: moving between modes of expression as a model for supervision. In H. Payne (Ed.) *Supervision of Dance Movement Psychotherapy. A Practitioner's Handbook.* London & New York: Routledge. 137–53.

Bownas, J. & Fredman, G. (Eds.) (2017). *Working with Embodiment in Supervision: A Systemic Approach.* London: Routledge.

Carroll, R. (2021). Embodied Intersubjectivity as online psychotherapy becomes mainstream. *Body, Movement and Dance in Psychotherapy: An International Journal for Theory, Research and Practice.* 16(1) 1–8.

Chesner, A. & Zografou, L. (Eds.) (2014). *Creative Supervision Across Modalities. Theory and Applications for Therapists, Counsellors and Other Helping Professionals.* London: Jessica Kingsley.

Frizell, C. (2019). Ecopsychology: working towards health and wellbeing in a world in which all matter matters. *International Festival of Mental Health and Wellbeing.* Royal Society of Arts, London, United Kingdom. 22–9. September 2019. [Lecture].

Frizell, C. (2012). Embodiment and the Supervisory Task. *Body, Movement and Dance in Psychotherapy: An International Journal for Theory, Research and Practice.* 7(4) 293–304.

Goldhahn, E. (2021). Being seen digitally: exploring macro and micro perspectives. *Body, Movement and Dance in Psychotherapy: An International Journal for Theory, Research and Practice.* 16(1) 87–100.

Panhofer, H., Payne, H., Meekums, B. & Parke T. (2011). The space between body and mind; Two models for group supervision. In S. Scoble (Ed.) *The Space Between: The Potential for Change. Selected Proceedings of the 10th European Arts Therapies Conference.* London: University of Plymouth Press (e-Book).

Payne, H. (Ed.). (2008). *Supervision of Dance Movement Psychotherapy.* London: Routledge.

Shohet, R. & Shohet, J. (2021). *In Love with Supervision. Creating Transformative Conversations.* Monmouth, UK: PCCS Books.

Turner, D. (2021). *Intersections of Privilege and Otherness in Counselling and Psychotherapy. Mockingbird.* London: Routledge.

Chapter 1

Perspective-Taking in Creative Supervision

Anna Chesner

Prologue

As I begin to write this chapter I am at the northernmost point in Europe, the Northern Cape in Norway, approaching the shortest day of the year. From this perspective, the horizon is vast and there is a different apprehension of the truth that the world is round. There is no sunrise or sunset, but an almost monochrome blue light for a couple of hours in the day.

To be located somewhere and somewhen is an embodied experience. I am in a different place than the everyday reality of my London consulting room. My eyes are focusing on a further horizon, and my lungs are filling with cleaner and cooler air. My heart rate is probably dropping in response to the still Arctic water around me, the vision of light reflected in the water and the subtle change of the diminishing winter light. In my imagination I can evoke the image and the felt sense of my workspace in London, the proportions and dimensions of that room, the creative props that inhabit the shelves on one wall and the angle of the chairs in relation to each other. I can also conjure imaginatively both the therapy clients and supervisees with whom I sit, talk, move, laugh and reflect.

This act of being in one place whilst imaginatively engaging with the felt sense of another place and time is at the heart of supervision. Whilst imagination itself is a sophisticated and creative mental activity, it is also an embodied act, through which the impact of the senses, the experience of being with the other, is re-evoked and then subjected to the particular light of reflection that takes place in the supervisory space. It is the purpose of this space to facilitate changes in perspective, for both supervisor and supervisee. Let's face it, the very term super-vision conjures up the possibility and desirability of changing perspective, of viewing our practice from a different place.

Creative methods used intentionally and hygienically help us to get *in touch* with the information of our senses and notice what has *touched* us. Supervision is a place to 'make sense' of our practice, and paying attention to our senses is an important part of this practice.

DOI: 10.4324/9781003034940-2

The Lens

As both practitioners and supervisors, we need to develop a varifocal lens. On the one hand, it is helpful to articulate a supervisory question or focus in the early stages of a supervisory conversation, e.g. 'I want to look at why I feel stuck with a particular client'. Having such a question helps to focus the lens of enquiry, in this example onto the therapeutic relationship, the current transference and countertransference experience. At the same time, the ability to take in the bigger picture might bring extra value to the enquiry, perhaps looking at the history of the work or the wider family and social setting of the client and the work. Certain agility in moving from the narrow to the wider focus will open the possibility of getting in touch with new information and playing with multiple perspectives. We use the term 'I see' to mean 'I understand'. Seeing in a varifocal way may deepen and refine our understanding.

In this chapter, I shall give examples through three vignettes that highlight the use of perspective-taking to develop a varifocal lens. In each case the supervisor uses the psychodramatic techniques of concretisation and working with role, in various combinations. Concretisation is the art of putting the inner world outside (Holmes, 1992; Chesner, 2019) through the use of tangible and visual objects, which can be moved around and re-configured as the perspective changes. Role work is the embodied process of stepping into the shoes (and the perspective) of the other (Chesner, ibid).

Example One: Role Reversal – Stepping into the Shoes of the Other

Role reversal is the core technique and building block of psychodrama, and to use it in an informed way it is important to understand the psychodramatic concept of role as the 'functioning form' the human being takes in any given situation (Moreno, 1961 in Fox, 1987: 62). In other words, a role is a way of being. Supervision is a space for reviewing our own way of being as practitioners and of deepening our understanding of our clients' ways of being within the contexts they find themselves in. By extension, we might also look at our own or our team's way of being in response to the wider picture.

Moreno, the founder of psychodrama, defined spontaneity as an adequate response to a new situation or a new response to an old situation (Goldman & Morrison, 1984: 6). It is not a fixed thing, like a personality type, but is always context-specific. So, in order to shed light on any perceived role, we need to expand our perspective and look at the role systemically, in context. What is the role a response to? A typical example of the importance of context emerges in this case.

> The supervisee, Sarah brings a concern about her new client, Mina's current situation.

This apparently anxious, self-effacing client is best understood when we widen our perspective to include the context of her longstanding relationship with a controlling, aggressive and alcoholic partner whom she recently left. Their destructive dance of roles makes even more sense when we further expand our perspective through the dimension of time and pay attention to the family-of-origin role of 'family skivvy' she developed from a young age. Mina learned as a child to take a back seat to others, to provide service to the wider household of brothers and parents, and to dismiss her own voice and needs.

She has recently left her abusive partner, but has immediately allied herself to a new man, one who at moments is described as kind and supportive, but who also seems, at least to Sarah, to be potentially another controller. Sarah's supervisory question is "Am I getting too involved in this case, am I falling into the role of rescuer or adviser, rather than therapist?"

The supervisor suggests some simple role work to explore the therapeutic relationship between Sarah and Mina in the light of this question. The supervisor's own thinking is to focus on eyes 3 and 4 of Hawkins and Shohet's seven-eyed model, the transference and countertransference relationship, and to bear in mind the wider context.

(Hawkins & Shohet, 2012)

SUPERVISOR: *Would you be interested in exploring this question through some role work?*

SUPERVISEE: *Yes, sure.*

SUPERVISOR: *So, let's bring this empty chair into the space and when you are ready I am going to ask you to take a seat in this empty chair, not as yourself but as your client, Mina. I will only address you as Mina whilst you are in this chair and you will respond in the first person as Mina. So, if you need to say something as yourself just come back to your own chair and your own role first. When you are ready…*

SARAH: *(moves across to the empty chair)*

SUPERVISOR: *Find your body posture as Mina, your way of sitting…*

SARAH: *(adjusts her position, letting her chest cave inwards, and holding her arms tight to her body and her feet together)*

SUPERVISOR: *Hello Mina, what are you wearing as you sit here?*

SARAH AS MINA: *A dress, kitten heels, cardigan.*

SUPERVISOR: *How long have you been coming to see Sarah?*

SARAH AS MINA: *Six weeks, I got referred through work. I've never done anything like this before. It's helping, Sarah helps me stop and think about things.*

SUPERVISOR: *Sarah wonders if she is too involved or tending to offer you advice, what do you think from your perspective?*

SARAH AS MINA: *I don't know…I notice that when I am in the session I see things more clearly, and I think, I must stand up for myself more. Then I go home and during the week I notice how I don't stand up for myself, at work, in relation to my ex, and with my current partner. And I catch myself thinking, Sarah's going to be disappointed. Like maybe I've failed a homework task!*

SUPERVISOR: *Thank you. Come back to your own role and chair, Sarah.*

SARAH (FROM HER OWN CHAIR): *Well that was interesting! I guess I am falling into that trap a bit. It's difficult in short term work, to try and achieve something without driving the process too much.*

SUPERVISOR: *So, what are you noticing, or taking from this?*

SARAH: *Well, sitting in Mina's shoes I got in touch with my own history, how I felt when I split up with my partner a while ago, and how I struggled to be strong in my own decision. It took us ages to really separate. I'm a bit ashamed of it really! Perhaps I'm trying to get Mina to be more decisive and assertive than I was myself. That's the thing that's hooked me in. I hadn't realised that until I sat there. I think I need to remind myself that this is her process. Of course, I want to support her, but I need to be careful not to push her to change more quickly than she can. I think I need to bear the frustration of her going at her own pace. That's helpful, I sensed there was something going on, but couldn't quite put my finger on it.*

Commentary

This example of a short intervention using role work demonstrates some key features of this method. First, the imaginative process of getting into the role is best approached through the body. Before speaking as Mina Sarah is encouraged to find her posture and to get a sense of how her client feels in her own skin and her own clothes. Only then does the interview-in-role begin. This is a matter of psychological hygiene, whereby the supervisor encourages clarity around the distinct roles and perspectives of the therapist–client dyad. Second, and linked to this, each role is located in space, marked by a chair, a cushion or even a piece of paper. This is similar to, but also distinct from the systemic practice of *interviewing the internalised other* (Sherbersky, 2014; Bond, 2017) a technique that seems to have been an adaptation of psychodramatic role work but crucially has lost the aesthetic and embodied emphasis of psychodramatic role work in terms of locating each role in space. In Sarah's case, embodying and speaking as her client put her in touch with how uncritically Mina accepted the therapist's interventions, characteristically criticising herself for not being good enough for the therapist. Moving back to her own role (located in her own chair), Sarah was able to engage with this information in a more self-questioning way and to make sense of the client's experience in the light of her own responsibilities as a therapist. Third, whilst holding the role of the client, and speaking as the client, she spontaneously contacted a personal memory of her own process of splitting from a partner. This was not articulated in the role of the client, but held on to, and brought back to her own role for discussion. Her counter-transferential identification with the role of 'woman breaking up from her partner' could be felt and understood through the role work. At the same time, the hygienic discipline of speaking from each role, in turn, and in its own place supported the psychological separation of what was her own and what was the client's. Finally, various aspects of context came to light through this short intervention: the pressure of short-term work on the practitioner; the contextual factor for the client of her historical role in the family, life with her ex; at work; and with her current partner. In each situation, faced with the expectations and needs of the other her response is to comply, disempower herself and keep quiet. This seems to be driven by an implicit belief that her place is to serve others and that she is 'less than'. Consequently, she faces the same problem in many areas of her life, which in turn tends to make her feel inadequate – also and crucially in terms of this session, in relation to the expectations of her therapist.

Example Two: Concretisation and Multiple Perspectives

The supervisee Bea is at a point in her developing practice where she wishes to devote a session to looking at her practice as a whole, areas that are developing, others that she would like to develop and others that seem to be receding. Her supervisory question is "How can I create a balance in the different areas of my professional life, what are my priorities and what steps might I need to take to create a sustainable creative practice?"

The supervisor invites her to map out the different "areas" she mentions, using a cushion on the floor to mark the location of each professional space, whether actual or emerging as a potential.

A network of areas emerges: her small one-to-one therapy practice; her new and growing creative consultation business; her intention to write and publish about that new field; her plan of eventually creating a training based on that developing business.

She is then asked to stand by each cushion in turn and notice what she gets in touch with. There is something about simply standing in one place at a time that allows her to fully focus on that area, knowing that the other areas have been marked, and can be attended to in due course. She begins with the one-to-one therapy practice. As she stands there she starts to talk about the setting where this work takes place, and some issues that have emerged with a receptionist. The story begins almost as an aside. As this problematic relationship comes into focus the supervisor asks her to choose an object to mark this person with a small object. She chooses a hedgehog figure. A story unfolds about casual boundaries and the negative impact on a client who chose to leave therapy as a direct consequence of their interaction with the receptionist. Bea reflects on whether and how she might take action to manage the relationship.

The next area she moves to is the cushion that represents her creative consultation business. This cushion is just two steps away from where she was standing, but as she arrives there inevitably her perspective changes, not only physically, but also mentally, emotionally and even ethically. She takes herself by surprise as she looks back at the cushion symbolising her private one-to-one practice and the little hedgehog figure representing the prickly presence at the threshold of that practice. From this new perspective her attitude shifts to something more critical and sceptical, and she asks in a much firmer voice than before, "Is that setting really appropriate for my practice? It's not acceptable. My practice deserves something better." It is a truism in psychodramatic practice that we know things in one role that we don't know in another. This applies not only to psychotherapeutic work but also within the frame of supervision. In this case we might say the supervisee perceives something from one perspective that she was unable or less able to see from another.

As the session develops, further insights emerge around the other areas of her professional life. She develops a clarity of plan around when and how to engage with her writing project and the steps required to develop a training. As she makes internal links between one area of her practice and another she marks these with bridges (cloths that link one cushion to another). These external, concretised symbols of an internal process remain in the supervision space as an anchor and visual focus for both supervisor and supervisee as they continue to discuss her situation and explore her options. The internal clarification of priorities, ideas and links is matched externally by the increasing level of detail in the concretised three-dimensional map or image that the supervisee creates. At the end of the session Bea reflects on the 'Aha' moment that occurred when she moved from the perspective of being in her one-to-one practice, to looking at it from outside. She also notes, that it was not only the shift in perspective but also the engagement and movement of her body through the space that released this clarity of thought.

Example Three: At the Threshold of Lockdown – Facing Change

The year 2020 brought with it unprecedented challenges for therapists and supervisors, as the global Covid-19 pandemic stopped us all in our habitual tracks and presented us with a significant challenge to our spontaneity. Here was a new situation, one where the simple embodied reality of being in a room with someone else became questionable and eventually, for a significant period, legally impossible. This novel challenge demanded a prompt response.

John, an experienced practitioner who comes for a one-off consultation reflects on the different responses he is confronted with as he offers his clients the possibility of continuing their therapy process online. This is shortly before the first lockdown, where there is still the possibility of careful face to face meetings. He has one client, Diane who is in training as a therapist and is being told by her university that the expectation is for all trainees to move their work to an online platform, but she is resistant to working remotely, whether as client with John or as trainee therapist.

John contrasts Diane's resistance to working online with another client's positive glee at the prospect. Fred works in IT and is generally 'avoidant' of the intimacy of relationship. He has been working well in therapy but relishes the opportunity to work through a medium that corresponds to his area of expertise and to finally be able to keep John at a distance.

John's supervisory question, relating to these contrasting cases emerges as "Where and why do I give way, and when and how do I hold firm?"

The supervision session itself is conducted via Zoom, which raises an additional question for us as supervisor and supervisee, of how transferable the psychodramatic action method of working with role is to the perspective and medium of online supervision.

John is directed initially to set up his space so there is enough room for him to embody three different roles, each in a distinctive location of its own. Role reversal as a technique is reliant on the proxemics of role, their spatial relationship with each other, and the embodied role relationship. With the constraints of a smaller space this matter of hygiene is especially important.

There are three roles on the Zoom stage: John the supervisee is in the middle. To his right is Diane, the therapy trainee with her resistance to all aspects of online working. To his left is Fred, raring to go into the online mode of working.

Then there is myself, an experienced supervisor in the early stages of my own steep learning curve in terms of adapting my entire practice (training, group and individual psychotherapy and supervision) to the online, potentially disembodied, experience of Zoom. I find myself wanting to pay special attention to the body and the embodied sense of relational dynamics.

I direct John to move to the location identified as marking Diane's role and to begin the work by focusing on the body. I ask him to find her physical, non-verbal gesture in response to the given context, i.e. her therapist, her college, potentially her government requiring a change from her, a change of the rules of engagement. John, standing, begins an agitated gesture that seems to be moving from the core of the body to the hands. I invite him to speak as Diane's agitation and the gesture develops into a fluttering, a pushing away and eventually a two-handed Stop gesture. The words that accompany this physical reaction are: "I'm furious, I'm at the end of my tether, it's all too much. Don't tell me what to do, I can't take it … life has been full of enough changes, my divorce, change of job, my big birthday. No! No more!"

I direct John back into his own role, with its own location, and to face the (empty) space where Diane's role is. I ask him what his response is to that gesture and those words, what it does to him, in the light of his supervisory question, about giving way or holding firm.

John responds in the direction of the role of Diane. He offers a gesture that is open, and solid and says:

"I have full sight of you – I can see your hands, but it's also important to see what is behind the gesture, and the entirety of you. I see and feel the resistance, but I also see what is only the current painful circumstance. Yes, it is hard to face change after change, one disruption after another, one challenge after another. On that basis, let's find a way to carry on working together, maybe at a physical distance face to face for as long as we are allowed, and then let's see, together."

I ask him to return to Diane's role and feel the impact of this gesture and these words. He does so, lowers his hands from the Stop gesture and says, "Yes, it feels good, I feel acknowledged, understood, and I am able to lower my own hands. I feel that you have recognised my limits."

I bring him back to his own role and ask him to face the other way, towards Fred, then to move into Fred's designated place in role reversal.

His posture in this role is loose and dismissive. There is a shrug of shoulder. He speaks fast, easily, casually. "Yes, I'm entirely comfortable with it, I'm working 24/7 online, I'm flexible, can see you any time. Just let me know when it suits you. Great that there is more flexibility now and we can all work remotely."

John, back in his own role laughs, hands on hips and responds, "Fred, I can see that there is a lot to like in this potential change, but there is something of real value in having a regular space that is predictable and brings structure to you in a world of change."

I interject as supervisor, "He seems to want to change the frame…what do you want to say to him about that?"

John continues, "Your time slot will be honoured and we will keep to that. This is a temporary arrangement during this time. I'm holding firm to that." He changes position, one foot comes forward in a stable stance, and he inclines his body more towards Fred. It looks somewhat martial, but not aggressive.

As supervisor I ask him to feel into that stance, and to give a message, not to Fred, but to himself from that new position. My expectation is that he will encourage himself to hold firm, to hold his authority in the face of Fred's casualness and attack on the frame. However, he surprises me with a very different message to self.

John hesitates, reflecting silently for a moment, then speaks. "Remember not to be too domineering, remember Fred's relationship with his own father, who is authoritarian and inflexible, dominant. I need to be careful. I've always tried not to replicate that relationship in the therapy up until now. That's important, don't lose sight of that!"

He changes the stance to be less oppositional, angling his body slightly away from Fred, and brings his front foot back. He nods.

I direct him to role reverse with Fred and take in the impact of these two stances.

He moves across to Fred's position and role, pauses a moment, then comments. "That was a bit threatening at first, but now you have stepped back I feel more relaxed and able to talk about it. Yes, the regularity of time has been helpful and important. I can see that."

After this double role encounter, I direct John to de-role the space and come back to his central position to reflect together on what he has discovered.

John notes that the work was powerful and helpful and that there was something honouring of each client to consider them simultaneously in this way and to note the very different significance of a potential change in the therapy frame for each of them. We note together which moments were key in the process. In terms of the work with Diane the embodied gesture he found in the role gave him direct access to her sense of vulnerability, threat and potential dysregulation and helped him empathise with the reality of her limits in adapting to change imposed from the outside. As a consequence, when he moved back to his own role and observed the gesture in his mind's eye he could both see the gesture itself and beyond it to the conditioning factors behind it. There was an interplay of perspectives both from within her experience and from his own position as her therapist with knowledge of her recent and less recent history. It was the combination of those perspectives that gave him more confidence in how he would respond to her, with flexibility and empathy.

The other key moment was when facing the role of Fred he gave his message to himself. There was something about the clarity of his implicit embodied message as he took up the martial stance towards Fred, and my invitation to feel into that and give himself a message, which enabled him to get in touch with so much of the client's history and the history of the therapy relationship. He was able to sense and identify the paternal countertransference and its potential impact on Fred and to fine-tune the response to one that was relationally adequate. I was reminded of how creative supervision gives us the opportunity to get back in touch with what we know already as practitioners, but have lost contact with. For me as a supervisor, such insights that come from the therapist's own knowledge and arise through the experience of the action methods offered can be the most satisfying.

Conclusion

I began writing this chapter towards the end of 2019 and finished it several months later. During the intervening time, the concepts of body, embodiment and perspective took on new dimensions in the light of the global pandemic. The wide horizon I was enjoying in December 2019 was exchanged for weeks of lockdown and physical isolation in my London flat. The embodied ritual of supervisees physically journeying to and from my consulting room for sessions changed to meeting via a flat-screen, each in our own home. We have now become accustomed to the small distortions of connectivity that impinge on the senses of myself and my supervisees. The whole notion of two peoples' body and breath in the same space became coloured by danger. That physical attunement in a shared space, which is such a natural, even unconscious, part of the supervisory process, now seems like the 'old normal'. Despite having returned to in-person practice, or a hybrid practice that combines in-person and online sessions, that normal has not yet been resumed. What a change in perspective at a collective and personal level!

What has remained consistent during this extraordinary time is the role of the imagination. This enables us to connect in the 'as if', bringing the supervisees' sessions in the 'there and then' into the 'here and now' of our encounter. Through the imagination, assisted at times by the techniques of concretisation and working with role, we are still able to subject their work to the light of shared reflection and tune into the world of information the body holds.

References

Bond, S. (2017). Supervision as a Cluster of Conversations. In J. Bownas and G. Fredman (Eds.) *Working with Embodiment in Supervision*. London: Routledge. 49–64.

Chesner, A. (2019). *One-to-One Psychodrama Psychotherapy Applications and Technique*. London: Routledge.

Goldman, E. & Morrison, D. (1984). *Psychodrama Experience & Process*. Iowa: Kendall/Hunt.

Hawkins, P. & Shohet, R. (2012). *Supervision in the Helping Professions* (4th edn). Maidenhead: Open University Press.

Holmes, P. (1992). *The Inner World Outside: Object Relations Theory and Psychodrama*. London: Routledge.

Moreno, J.L. (1961). The Role Concept, A Bridge between Psychiatry and Sociology. In J. Fox (Ed.) (1987). *The Essential Moreno: Writings on Psychodrama, Group Method, and Spontaneity*. New York: Springer. 60–66.

Sherbersky, H. (2014). Integrating Creative Approaches within Family Therapy Supervision. In A. Chesner and L. Zografou (Eds.) *Creative Supervision Across Modalities*. London: Jessica Kingsley. 89–109.

Chapter 2

The Dialogical Dance

A Relational Embodied Approach to Supervision

Yeva Feldman

Introduction

> If you cannot find it in your own body, where will you go in search of it?
> (The Upanishads, 2011)

Turning to our bodies for answers is an essential practice when training and supervising dance movement psychotherapists (DMPs). In fact, to be embodied and work with embodiment is a relevant practice for any creative, holistic and relational practitioner. Central to my embodied relational approach to supervision is the belief that listening to our bodies, developing and strengthening our body knowledge and engaging in a deeply relational way will give trainee therapists the tools to become embodied relational practitioners. It is vital to keep in mind that although the focus of this chapter is on supervision and the supervisee, the most important recipient and beneficiary of this approach is the client. It heightens the DMP trainee's embodied empathy for their clients; it strengthens the trainee's ability to use their body as a resource, providing the knowledge to support their clients to do the same; it deepens the DMP trainee's ability to be with their clients and to dance dialogically with them, metaphorically and literally. This supervision is an integral part of a dance movement psychotherapy training programme that promotes the development of embodied relational practitioners. This is also the author's own supervision approach developed over many years of educating and supervising trainees.

I am grateful to all my supervisees, past and present, for their collaboration and contribution to this method of supervision. I am especially thankful for the supervisees who have given their consent to be included in this chapter. All data from vignettes are pseudonymised.

Supervising Trainees

Supervision during training involves specific challenges and complexities. Trainees often have their first encounter with supervision during their

DOI: 10.4324/9781003034940-3

training. Inevitably this involves an initial imbalance of power between supervisor and trainee which is further heightened when supervision is embedded within an academic institution, involving assessments and course requirements. They may also have had previous negative and shame-inducing experiences within education which will have influenced a trainee's learning style and their ability to receive feedback (Carroll & Gilbert, 2005). New trainees need to feel safe in order to bring their fears, uncertainties, struggles and vulnerabilities to supervision. They require more encouragement and positive feedback. They will often focus on a 'right and wrong' paradigm with a fear of 'making mistakes'. To make the shift towards curiosity requires supervisors to be sensitive to power dynamics and to encourage mutuality in the relationship (Hawkins & Shohet, 2012). A reparative learning environment is enhanced through genuine mutual dialogue with the supervisor and with peers.

Supervising DMP trainees using movement and embodiment brings another layer of relating and reflection. We are not only communicating through words. We are engaging on a body-to-body level of communication. Listening and paying attention to their bodies give DMP trainees a deeper awareness and understanding of their own and their clients' experience. Movement in supervision provides opportunities to discover and practice embodied resources as well as the embodied relationship. Emphasis on movement in supervision can promote a sense of security within one's body, fostering a greater openness to experience (Federman, 2011). I found this to be especially true and effective when working with supervisees online, as the vignette below demonstrates:

> *During an online supervision session, I had asked everyone to focus inwardly, and move in response to their inner bodily experience. We all moved in our own spaces viewed through the screen. There was one supervisee who wasn't moving. Her back was to the camera and I couldn't 'see' her. However, I did have a bodily response to her embodiment. I felt tense, cold and my breath became shallow. I used my own body felt response to inquire about her experience. She resonated with my somatic experience and said she felt frozen with shame. The supervisee realised this wasn't to do with her clients, but rather with her fear of being criticised by an authority figure. She described a negative experience involving her presenting something of which she felt proud to her class only to have her teacher pick it apart until there was nothing good left. The shame and fear of revealing what she was proud of lived in her body and impacted her experience in supervision. She intended to bring a positive experience from her clinical practice to supervision, but she became paralysed with shame. Once we got to the source of her embodiment, with support and encouragement, she was able to find her own somatic response (fuller breaths, grounding, shaking off and releasing movements) and received support from the group. This reparative experience*

allowed her to stay with what she felt proud of and share it openly with the group. By following the supervisee's movements and embodying her shift from fear to support, the whole group moved beyond their own screens into each other's virtual spaces to connect with and meet one another genuinely and deeply. I asked the group to follow the supervisee's example and share an aspect of their clinical work of which they felt most proud. This invited a celebration of each supervisee and the jubilant witness of their triumph – not something commonly focused on in supervision.

Group Supervision

The above group vignette illustrates the power of group supervision. Group supervision offers rich interpersonal and experiential learning and promotes kinship and mutuality which is especially useful for trainees. It allows trainees to share ideas from multiple perspectives and offers a broader system of support for individuals in the group. There is evidence that groups that foster working relationally enhance authenticity, connectivity and genuinely shared understanding (Wyatt, 2013). As seen in the vignette above, attending to bodily sensing in group supervision can include moments of deep connection amongst those present (Madison, 2004). For these reasons, group supervision is favoured when working with DMP trainees.

An Embodied Relational Approach

My embodied relational approach to clinical practice and supervision integrates Gestalt therapy (GT) with dance movement psychotherapy (DMP) (Feldman, 2016, 2017, 2021). Both Gestalt Therapy and Dance Movement Psychotherapy are process-oriented, experiential, relational and holistic disciplines (Perls, 1992; Joyce & Sills, 2014; Levy, 1988). Each approach focuses on awareness, a non-verbal knowing of 'what is' (Yontef, 1993). Awareness is sensory, always taking place in the present and constantly changing (Perls, 1973). I believe that embodied and experiential exploration in supervision can enhance self-reflection. Developing self-awareness in supervision ultimately enables supervisees to respond to their clients genuinely, collaboratively and flexibly. Supervision that is experiential, embodied and process oriented provides a greater opportunity for supervisees to expand their self-awareness and creative responsiveness to their clients.

Bodily experience is fundamental to both GT and DMP. Awareness begins with bodily sensations (Perls, 1992). Bodily awareness is the gateway to authentic expression (Chodorow, 2016) and a deep embodied understanding of others (Sletvold, 2015). In both approaches, a focus on one's own body-felt sensations is used to understand unspoken communication from clients and supervisees. In DMP, there is a greater emphasis on the use of movement as a phenomenological method of investigation and a way of establishing a therapeutic relationship (Chace, 1993). In both Gestalt Therapy and Dance Movement Psychotherapy, there is a deep-rooted belief that (bodily) experience is inherently relational and that our relationships are fundamentally embodied (Spagnuolo-Lobb, 2015; Panhofer, Payne, Meekums & Parke, 2011; Kepner, 2003). This core belief underpins all my clinical and supervisory relationships.

Embodiment in Supervision

To be embodied means owning body experience as self-experience. How we experience our bodies is how we experience ourselves (Kepner, 2003). We feel, think and exist in the world through our physical being. 'Our kinaesthetic body is always present' (Panhofer, Payne, Meekums & Parke, 2011:10). Movement is the language of our bodies which DMPs utilise to promote awareness, expression and communication. We process, reflect, communicate and express ourselves through our bodies. There is recognition that developing trust in one's bodily sense of self in supervision leads to the development of meaningful interaction with clients (Lopez, 2008). Supervisors from different modalities have come to realise the necessity for incorporating experiential and embodied approaches in supervision (Chesner & Zografou, 2014; Bownas & Fredman, 2017; Shohet & Shohet, 2020; Sletvold, 2015).

There are several different ways of using embodiment in supervision. One is through a focus on bodily sensations and being open to the wisdom of one's body (Meekums, 2008). This deepens the kinaesthetic knowing of personal counter-transferential and unconscious material on a body level (Panhofer, Payne, Meekums & Parke, 2011; Wyman- McGinty, 2008). It also promotes a greater understanding and heightened sensitivity to clients' somatic experiences (Wyman- McGinty, 2008). By focusing on bodily felt experience, supervisees learn to trust, attend and become fully present to themselves and their clients. They become adept at finding answers in their own bodies.

Movement is a multifaceted resource used in DMP supervision. Movement is the way we express ourselves and interact in the world. Genuine and authentic movement gives meaning to our internal experiences which can then be communicated and met (Kepner, 1993). Exploration through movement improvisation allows supervisees to express what it is like being with clients and deepens their ability to enter the client's world (Federman & Gaber, 2008). By moving with others when reflecting on clinical material, supervisees deepen their understanding of movement as communication and a non-verbal form of relating (Butté & Hoo, 2014). Movement enhances the experience of dialogical relating, and this enables supervisees to have a greater embodied understanding, thus developing their capacity for relational depth with their clients.

The Dialogical Dance in Supervision

Buber's 'I thou' attitude (Buber, 1970) is the foundation of a dialogical relationship in Gestalt Therapy. It is this relationship that is believed to be the source of healing for clients (Hycner, 1995). To be dialogical, a therapist (or supervisor) needs to bring all of herself into the present moment with the other and let go of goals and techniques. It involves authenticity, genuine unreserved dialogue and affirmation of the uniqueness of the other (Hycner, 1995). Being dialogical means experiencing the phenomenological world of the other without judgment (Buber, 1970). The dialogical dance is an embodiment of the rhythmic, back and forth, deeply felt understanding of the other's experience while retaining one's own. Marion Chace (1993) contacted the most unreachable patients by picking up on their non-verbal expression in her own body and reflecting it back to them in her dance. She knew implicitly what has been supported by contemporary neuroscience, which we can understand each other through body-to-body knowing (Gallese, 2009).

Using dance as a metaphor to describe a deeply felt relationship highlights the parallels between dance and relationships (Hycner, 1995; McFerran & Finlay, 2018; Spognuolo-Lobb, 2015). This can be illustrated by the relational dance between supervisees and the supervisor. Moving with supervisees in synchrony and with a common rhythm promotes the experience of deep connection and inclusion (Schmais, 1985; Ammaniti & Ferrari, 2013). The nature of the dialogical dance in supervision touches upon innate, non-verbal, deeply held knowledge about self and others and refines this with new embodied relational knowing. This is what the supervisor offers supervisees through their dance together. Practicing these relational dance steps in supervision prepares supervisees for an embodied dialogical relationship with clients.

However, the dance between supervisees and clients has many potential challenges. There are new steps to learn and different dance styles to pick up. Supervisees must learn to wait, attune and pick up on their clients' moves; stay curious and follow their clients' dance steps even when it is not clear where they are going; persist with the unknown dance, trusting themselves; and know when they are becoming swept away in their clients' dance or when they have interrupted their clients' flow. In supervision, I address these literal and metaphorical interruptions through embodied explorations. These embodied investigations focus on three main techniques: increasing awareness through body felt sensations, embodying clients to heighten the experience of inclusion and kinesthetic empathy and movement improvisation in response to emergent themes.

Increasing Awareness Through Focus on Felt Sense

Bodily awareness or focusing on the 'felt sense' (Gendlin, 1981: 32) in supervision enables trainees to listen to and receive answers from their bodies, accessing alternative ways of knowing. A felt sense is a physical experience that is not easy to describe in words (Gendlin, 1981) but can be 'symbolized precisely- in very diverse ways' (Lopez, 2008: 236). It is 'an internal aura that encompasses everything you feel and know about the given subject at a given time' that comes to you in a single bodily feeling (Gendlin, 1981: 32). Focusing on bodily felt sensations in supervision enables supervisees to build and access their kinaesthetic knowledge.

At the beginning of each supervision session, I ask supervisees to attend to their present embodiment and to focus on their bodily felt sensations in the here and now. They may follow their bodily flow of experiencing without any identifiable issues. The process involves them identifying and staying with an unclear sensation until they feel they have 'received' the bodily message (Gendlin, 1981: 45). I ask them to find a word or phrase that resonates and to continue to move, following and clarifying the received bodily message. I then ask them to find the polarity or a reparative response to their bodily message. This is to activate and heighten their bodily know-ledge and resources. Through this exploration, supervisees often find their own responses and solutions to their original bodily message or issue. When we identify something painful in our bodies, it is within our bodies that we can also discover the method of healing (Spognoulo-Lobb, 2015). Somatic resources are our bodies' intersubjective embodied reparative tool kit. These resources can be identified, strengthened and renewed (Buckley, Punkanen, & Ogden, 2018). These explorations are often poignant and transformational. They often bridge the personal and professional and dir-ectly address core beliefs.

In supervision, Linda, a second-year trainee, began moving focusing on her felt sense, and noticed she felt 'off balance'. As she explored this sensa-tion further, she described feeling 'pulled in' and that she couldn't find her ground. I asked the group to mirror and embody her movements of being 'off balance' and 'pulled in'. This enabled the group to have an embodied understanding of her experience and gave Linda some additional experien-tial data. Group members expressed feeling tense, out of control and anx-ious. Linda related these feelings to herself and her placement setting. When embodying Linda's movements, I found myself feeling resistant. I didn't want to move and felt a need to say 'no'. Understanding that this was emer-ging from the 'embodied field' (Kepner, 2003), I shared this with Linda and the group. Linda acknowledged that she found it hard to set bound-aries and to say 'no' in this placement setting (and more generally). I asked Linda to explore what she needed, to feel more grounded and balanced. This facilitated an improvisation in which Linda focused on feeling her feet on the floor, activating her strength in a firm and grounded stance, and finding her voice. She experimented with saying 'no' while staying in a grounded stance and found that she felt more centred and boundaried.

This vignette highlights that following bodily experience can support clarification of experience, identifying obstacles as well as solutions. It also demonstrates that the body felt sensations of group members and supervisor can assist supervisees in clarifying and facilitating their emerging process. It illustrates that movement and words that arise from our bodies can promote integration. The role of the supervisor is to listen to their own body and provide space for exploration and relational support.

Embodying Clients

Embodying clients involves metaphorically bringing clients into the supervision space by simulating how they move and interact with others. The rationale, supported by neuroscience, is that individuals can be understood through embodied simulation, a shared body state, when doing the same action as the other (Gallese, 2009). Supervisees come to have a better understanding of their clients through sensing and reflecting on their own bodily experience when embodying their clients in supervision. Moving as their clients in supervision requires trainees to develop highly tuned observational capacity, the ability to synchronise with their clients' movements and non-verbal expression and the ability to stay centred in their own bodily sense of self. By embodying clients in supervision, supervisees gain not only a better understanding of their clients but also a heightened capacity for Buber's (1967) notion of inclusion.

Buber's (ibid) concept of inclusion, an existential approach to empathy, encompasses a bodily process. 'The therapist must feel the other side, the patients' side of the relationship, as a bodily touch to know how the patient feels it' (ibid, 1967: 173). Inclusion is the movement towards understanding the client's experience, from the client's point of view, while remaining centred (Hycner, 1995). When supervisees embody clients in supervision, they are able to understand their client's experience from the client's perspective, while retaining a bodily sense of self. In addition, this strengthens their ability to identify and differentiate their client's experience from their own.

> Sophia, a second-year trainee, struggled to understand an angry young client whom she described as 'challenging'. In Sophia's culture, anger was not an emotion that was permitted or expressed openly. In her culture it was 'wrong' to express anger. In supervision she realised that she held in her anger and directed it towards herself, in the form of self-criticism. She said that no one had ever told her that it was okay to express anger. She realised that this was why she felt stuck when her client expressed anger. I asked her to embody this client and bring her client into the room. As the client, she stamped her feet, punched and kicked. She shouted 'no' and then stopped. She said that she felt anxious from doing this as this expression was taboo in her culture. The group and I gave her permission and

encouragement by accompanying her in her movement exploration with our own 'angry' movements. This enabled her to continue to explore her client's anger and at the same time get in touch with her own. When she finished, she was surprised to find that she felt empowered and nothing terrible had happened to her or to others. As a result of her client embodiment, she was able to understand that her client wasn't challenging her, but needed space and encouragement to express her anger, as she herself had done in the supervision space.

From an embodied perspective, 'culture is manifested in our bodies moving in relation to each other in a developed pattern' (Clemmens & Bursztyn, 2003: 16). By embodying her client, Sophia directly faced and challenged her embodied cultural beliefs around anger. It was only by embodying her client's anger and experiencing it for herself that Sophia was able to feel and understand her client's experience and move towards inclusion.

Movement Improvisation in Supervision

Movement improvisation blends authentic, meaning-making movement with spontaneity and embracing the unknown. It's about creating '...an ongoing present from the world of possibilities at any given moment' (Sheets Johnstone, 1981: 399). Movement improvisation involves playing, embracing uncertainty, taking risks and experimenting. When improvising 'there are no mistakes, only possibilities' (Kossak, 2020: 67). The nature of movement improvisation makes it a valuable tool in supervision. It promotes experiential bodily learning that enhances the supervisees' body knowledge, ability to tolerate uncertainty, to respond authentically and be open to multiple possibilities. It counteracts their need to 'get it right' and prepares them for collaborative play. Movement improvisation is a method for developing a sense of bodily centredness in one's self while maintaining genuine contact with others. Most importantly, it is a way that supervisees can explore challenges and find their own solutions.

Beginning trainees often describe issues related to boundaries. In this group, supervisees described feeling invaded, unsafe, powerless and distressed in relation to clients and placement settings. I suggested a movement improvisation focusing on body boundaries using their own kinesphere (the space around their body) as a starting point. They moved as if they had bubbles around them. I suggested they explore the nature of their boundary/bubble further in their improvisation (such as what material their bubble was made from, how they made contact from their bubble, who could come in and who couldn't). I asked the group to share their improvised creations one at a time. The following are a few examples:

> *Sarah said her bubble was made out of brick. It was impenetrable to ensure that she felt safe. When I asked her to make contact with another group member with her bubble, she realised she had to step outside her bubble to make contact, leaving her feeling vulnerable and exposed. She realized that she oscillated between putting up a brick wall, not letting anyone in, or being completely unprotected. Using movement improvisation, I asked her to explore a different kind of bubble where she could feel safe and have contact at the same time. She adapted her bubble to include a window and a door, so that she could choose to make contact at her own pace. This enabled her to feel more available to her clients. Janet on the other hand, said that her bubble was made out of silk scarves, colourful and flowing. Using movement improvisation, I asked her to explore what happened to her bubble when in relationship. She realised that her colourful, open bubble did not offer her much protection and choice. I asked her to continue moving and make adaptations to her bubble that would allow her to be more choiceful. She added an inner layer of transparent resilient plastic, which she reported not only offered her a greater sense of her own boundary, but paradoxically allowed her to be more open and available to her clients.*

This vignette highlights the nature of movement improvisation as a phenomenological method of investigation and exploration. Through movement improvisation, supervisees were able to investigate and heighten their awareness of the constraints in their personal boundaries and explore new possibilities in their contact boundaries through imagery and movement. This movement improvisation allowed them to explore the problem as well as the solution on a bodily level resulting in positive changes to their relationships with clients.

Embodied Relational Supervision Online

Due to the Covid-19 pandemic, there were several long periods of time during which supervision took place online. Although we were all in our separate spaces literally and on the screen, we were still able to work in an embodied relational way. In some ways, I was able to 'see' more of each individual in their home space. For example, it became apparent, through what one supervisee was wearing and how she was moving, that she had no heating. When I investigated further, I learned that she was on her own in a house that she usually shared with others, struggling to pay for the heating and food. This prompted another supervisee to offer to take a heater to her and other spontaneous expressions of support. It was incredibly touching to witness the level of group support for this supervisee. This wouldn't have been something I saw if we met in person. In addition, some supervisees felt safer and more contained working online and were therefore able to delve deeper into their embodied experience. Paradoxically, I have found working remotely often heightened my body responses, perhaps because my other senses were less active. Working remotely where the body of the supervisor still has a central role and where the supervisees maintain focus on body awareness, move together in synchrony and mirror each other's movements, creates and preserves the embodied relational connection (Engelhard & Furlager, 2021).

Concluding Thoughts

The main premise of my embodied relational approach is that listening to one's body and a deeply felt dialogic relationship are fundamentally healing (Hycner, 1995; Levy 1988). In supervision, a relational embodied approach is uniquely placed to prepare trainees to help others reconnect to their body wisdom within a reparative relationship. This approach prepares trainees to 'dance dialogically' with clients. Focusing on body felt sensations in supervision enables supervisees to listen, trust and use this bodily information to inform their dance. Embodying clients accelerates the development of deep embodied empathy, enabling supervisees to be open to the uniqueness of their clients and to engage with them as they are. Movement improvisation prepares supervisees for working collaboratively, authentically, flexibly and creatively. This facilitates a dance that is spontaneous, playful and full of multiple possibilities. Central to trainees understanding of how to be therapists evolves from being supervisees. Supervisees can learn how to be relational embodied practitioners by experiencing this approach for themselves in supervision.

Acknowledgement

My heartfelt gratitude goes to Phil Joyce for his ongoing support and help with this chapter.

References

Ammaniti, M. & Ferrari, P. (2013). Vitality affects in Daniel Stern's thinking – A psychological and neurobiological perspective. *Infant Mental Health Journal*, 34(5): 367–75. DOI: 10.1002/imhj.21405

Bownas, J. & Fredman, G. (Eds.) (2017). *Working with Embodiment in Supervision: A Systemic Approach*. Abingdon: Routledge.

Buber, M. (1967). *A Believing Humanism: Gleanings*. New York: Simon & Schuster.

Buber, M. (1970). *I and Thou*. New York: Scribner's Sons (Originally published 1923).

Buckley, T., Punkanen, M., & Ogden, P. (2018). The role of the body in fostering resilience: sensorimotor psychotherapy perspective. *Body, Movement and Dance in Psychotherapy: An International Journal for Theory, Research and Practice*, 13(4): 225–33. DOI: 10.1080/17432979.2018.1467344

Butté, C. & Hoo, F. (2014). Embodiment and movement in supervision: An integration of theories and techniques from body-oriented, movement-based psychotherapy and creative supervision. In A. Chesner & L. Zografou (Eds.). *Creative Supervision Across Modalities*. London: Jessica Kingsley. 127–44.

Carroll, M. & Gilbert, M.C. (2005). *On Being a Supervisee: Creating Learning Partnerships*. London: Vukani Publishing.

Chace, M. (1993). Techniques for the use of dance as a group therapy. In S.L. Sandel, S. Chaiklin & A. Lohn (Eds.). *Foundations of dance/movement therapy: The life and work of Marian Chace*. Maryland: The Marian Chace Memorial Fund of the American Dance Therapy Association. 204–9.

Chesner, A. & Zografou, L. (Eds.) (2014). *Creative supervision across modalities*. London: Jessica Kingsley.

Chodorow, J. (2016). Dance Therapy: Motion and Emotion. In S. Chaiklin & H. Wengrower (Eds.). *The art and science of Dance/ Movement Therapy: Life is dance* (2nd edn.). New York: Routledge. 53–74.

Clemmens, M.C. & Bursztyn, A. (2003). Culture and body: A phenomenological and dialogic inquiry. *The British Gestalt Journal*, 12(1):15–21.

Engelhard, E.S. & Furlager, A.Y. (2021). Remaining held: dance/movement therapy with children during lockdown. *Body, Movement and Dance in Psychotherapy*, 16(1): 73–86. DOI: 10.1080/17432979.2020.1850525

Federman, D.J. (2011). Kinaesthetic change in the professional development of Dance Movement Therapy trainees. *Body, Movement and Dance in Psychotherapy*, 6(3): 195–214. DOI: 10.1080/17432979.2010.545190

Federman, D.J. & Gaber, L.B. (2008). Supervision in dance movement therapy: a proposed model for trainees. In H. Payne (Ed.). *Supervision of Dance Movement Psychotherapy: A Practitioner's Handbook*. East Sussex: Routledge. 49–60.

Feldman, Y. (2016). How body psychotherapy influenced me to become a dance movement psychotherapist. *Body, Movement and Dance in Psychotherapy*, 11(2–3): 103–13. DOI: 10.1080/17432979.2015.1095802

Feldman, Y. (2017). Gestalt and dance movement psychotherapy in adults with eating disorders: Moving towards integration through practice and research. In H. Payne (Ed.). *Essentials of Dance Movement Psychotherapy: International Perspectives on Theory, Research and Practice*. New York: Routledge. 83–98.

Feldman, Y. (2021). Building resilience: Developing somatic and relational resources in a Gestalt Movement Therapy group for women with borderline personality disorder and histories of profound trauma. In A. Chesner & S. Iykou (Eds.). *Trauma in the Creative and Embodied Therapies: When Words Are Not Enough*. New York: Routledge. 80–91.

Gallese, V. (2009). Mirror neurons, embodied simulation and the neural basis of social identification. *Psychoanalytic Dialogues: The International Journal of Relational Perspectives*, 19(5): 519–36. DOI: 10.1080/10481880903231910

Gendlin, E.T. (1981). *Focusing*. New York: Bantam Books.

Hawkins, A. & Shohet, R. (2012). *Supervision in the Helping Professions* (4th edn.). Maidenhead: Open University Press.

Hycner, R. (1995). The dialogic ground. In R. Hycner & L. Jacobs (Eds.). *The Healing Relationship in Gestalt Therapy*. New York, NY: The Gestalt Journal Press. 3–29.

Joyce, P., & Sills, C. (2014). *Skills in Gestalt Counselling & Psychotherapy* (3rd edn.). London: Sage.

Kepner, J.I. (1993). *Body Process: Working with the Body in Psychotherapy*. San Francisco: Jossey-Bass.

Kepner, J.I. (2003). The embodied field. *The British Gestalt Journal*, 12(1): 6–14.

Kossak, M.S. (2009). Therapeutic attunement: A transpersonal view of expressive arts therapy. *The Arts in Psychotherapy*, 36(1): 13–18. DOI: 10.1016/j.aip.2008.09.003

Levy, F.J. (1988). *Dance Movement Therapy: A Healing Art*. Reston: American Alliance for Health, Physical Education, Recreation and Dance.

Lopez, S.M. (2008). The felt sense in psychotherapy supervision. *The Folio*, 21(1): 226–37.

Madison, (2004). Focusing-oriented supervision in K. Tudor & M. Worrall (Eds.). *Freedom to Practice: Person Centred Approaches to Supervision*. Ross-on-Wye: PCCS Books. 133–52.

McFerran, K.S. & Finlay, L. (2018). Resistance as a 'dance' between client and therapist. *Body, Movement and Dance in Psychotherapy*, 13(2): 114–27. DOI: 10.1080/17432979.2018.1448302

Meekums, B. (2008). Spontaneous symbolism in clinical supervision: Moving beyond logic. In H. Payne (Ed.). *Supervision of Dance Movement Psychotherapy: A Practitioner's Handbook*. East Sussex: Routledge. 18–32.

Panhofer, H., Payne, H., Meekums, B., Parke, T. (2011). Dancing, moving and writing in clinical supervision? Employing embodied practices in psychotherapy supervision. *The Arts in Psychotherapy*, 38(1): 9–16. DOI: 10.1016/j.aip.2010.10.001

Perls, F.S. (1973). *The Gestalt Approach and Eyewitness to Therapy*. New York: Bantam.

Perls, L. (1992). *Living at the Boundary*. Highland, NY: The Gestalt Journal Press.

Schmais, C. (1985). Healing process in group dance therapy. *American Journal of Dance Therapy*, 8: 17–36.

Spagnuolo-Lobb, M. (2015). The body as a "vehicle" of our being in the world. Somatic experience in Gestalt therapy. *British Gestalt Journal*, 24 (2): 21–31.

Sheets Johnstone, M. (1981). Thinking in movement. *The Journal of Aesthetics and Art Criticism*, 39(4): 399–407. DOI: 10.2307/430239

Shohet, R. & Shohet, J. (2020). *In Love with Supervision: Creating Transformative Conversations*. Wyastone: PCCS Books.

Sletvold, J. (2015). Embodied empathy in psychotherapy: Demonstrated in supervision. *Body, Movement and Dance in Psychotherapy*, 10(2): 82–93. DOI: 10.1080/17432979.2014.971873

The Upanishads (2011). The Marian Chance Foundation Bookmark Project. https://adta.org/MCF_Bookmark_Project.

Wyatt, G. (2013). Group relational depth. In R. Knox, D. Murphy, S. Wiggens & M. Cooper (Eds.). *Relational Depth: New Perspectives and Developments*. London: Palgrave Macmillan. 101–13.

Wyman-McGinty, W. (2008). The contribution of authentic movement in supervising dance movement therapists. In H. Payne (Ed.). *Supervision of Dance Movement Psychotherapy: A Practitioner's Handbook*. East Sussex: Routledge. 89–102.

Yontef, G.M. (1993). *Awareness, Dialogue & Process: Essays on Gestalt Therapy*. New York, NY: The Gestalt Journal Press.

Chapter 3

Multimodal and Liminal Perspectives (MLP)

The Role of Liminality in the Dynamic of the Supervisory Relationship

Bryn Jones

It was 1987 and I was living in Liverpool and involving, losing and growing myself in the city's independent, fractious and experimental theatre scene. I was staying just outside the city centre and one day found myself walking along a familiar street. This street when walked downwards took me into the city and onward towards the river. Turning around and travelling back up hill, it took me home. On this familiar path that day, I spotted something unfamiliar: a small A-frame sign with the words *Stone Field*. To the left of the sign, a wide opening gaped, a surprising gap amongst the otherwise uninterrupted line of boarded-up shopfronts. Staring in to the gloom, I discerned a long and cavernous corridor. Perhaps some promise of light at its end? I stepped in. Walking inside, my eyes gradually adjusted to the shadowy half-light and noticed art deco tiles lining the walls. Many were cracked, broken and missing. Some still in place, glinting. At the corridor's end is a vast open empty space. A quiet but fulsome light falling from above, criss-crossed by the remains of a skeletal iron roof frame, hanging and suspended over head. On the floor and occupying the space almost in its entirety lay a carefully crafted square of seemingly perfect and certainly luminous white stones. They hummed iridescent. They took my breath away. I stood momentarily transfixed. They drew me towards them. Irresistible. I found myself tracing their perfect edge pristine. My foot falls describing an angular circumambulation. I felt away. I felt other. I felt alone. As I neared the completion of my walking circuit, something stirred in the corner of the space. In the shadows, seemingly squatting, was a man. Watching. In fact he was sitting on a very low bench smoking a very thinly rolled cigarette. He asked me what I thought and told me that *Stone Field* was made by him and that he'd been journeying and making things like this as part of his walks: as memories, markings, histories and echoes. I chatted for a while and left. I walked up the hill, homewards. I later told some friends about the *Stone Field* and the man in the corner of the room. Finally I walked back down to see it again for myself. The pavement was bare. The A-frame sign was gone. The opening, if it ever was, was now shuttered and anonymous along the abandoned row of buildings. I wondered if I'd dreamt it.

DOI: 10.4324/9781003034940-4

I regard that experience as marking the beginning of a long and recurring line of interest that I've since followed. It involves the act of walking and moving and the choosing and gathering and placing of objects in sequences. I've been incorporating such activities initially, into my theatre and performance work, my spiritual practice and most recently in my therapeutic and supervisory practice. The method that I write about here is part of this practice lineage, and it reaches back, in my mind at least, to that day and that serendipitous encounter with the British land artist Richard Long.

Introduction

In this chapter, I aim to introduce and outline a new supervisory method which I am calling Multimodal and Liminal Perspectives (MLP). In this, I will be reflecting upon and drawing from my developing practice as a supervisor; the praxis that has fostered the constituent parts of this method and which has led to the formulation of this as a singular idea. I supplement this by occasional comment on the nature of the supervisory relationship and notions of co-creative and/or collaborative approaches in supervision. In exploring the intersubjective elements which underscore and inform the process, I am seeking to guide the attention of the reader to both the genesis of this multimodal method and key practice points for those wishing to try the method for themselves. I will reference the work of ethnographer and folklorist Arnold van Gennep whose *Rites of Passage* (1960) informs the method's basic ritual structure. To acknowledge the relationship and dialogue between different and discrete aspects of the technique, I will also consider the method from multimodal and intersubjective perspectives. In this, I will turn to the work of the psychoanalytic theorist Daniel Stern (Stern, 2018). I hope this will helpfully contextualise and further clarify the approaches I have drawn on in developing and refining my initial ideas.

On the Ways of Being a Supervisor and Supervising

In many ways, supervision remains an ever-unfolding mystery to me. This I notice is part of its enduring appeal as a live and sustaining part of my own practice: its elusiveness. The fact that in my role as supervisor, I can never fully grasp or hold in its entirety that which the supervisee might seek to bring. As supervisors, therefore, we are always being called upon to reach towards something just beyond our grasp. To work with those uncertainties Keats cursorily referred to as 'negative capability' (Keats, 1817: 277) and to draw upon intuitive imaginings in some attempt to make up for the inevitable lack of a fully comprehensive picture or script. And so, we're always with the gap, the absence, the discrepant and the incomplete and simultaneously sensing that it is right there, in that in-between space, that something new and other and easily overlooked might appear. And that through my exploring this with my supervisee, a beneficial new perspective might be forged.

In being a supervisor and supervising, we are inherently considering the supervisee and the nature of the supervisory encounter. It is within these intersubjective realms that the work occurs. In our meeting, our working and our being together, we might discover important links to notions of play: the shared experience of something new, unfamiliar and perhaps surprising coming to light. There is a dawning awareness of the immediate effect this process exerts. And then the question it carries, of what to do, think and feel about the matter to hand – the supervisory issue. These intersubjectivities involve both the personal and the shared, the nuance of embodied experience and the interplay of imagery.

> The three processes of 'letting happen', 'considering' and 'confronting oneself with' all emerge in the dialectic between the conscious and unconscious and within the therapeutic and supervisory relationship.
>
> (Perry, 2005: 193)

The emergence and constellation of these discrete components gradually define the quality and the scope of the supervisory relationship. Once active these elements can support both supervisor and supervisee in their individual and shared ventures.

In my own practice to date, I have noticed that the MLP method benefits from a similarly playful approach. Not a play that is frivolous or superficial but one that retains a lightness of touch and a capacity to wonder so as to enable and actualise a truly explorative and experimental process. One that allows for, perhaps even encourages, a sense of an embodied intuition. Although it may rightly be the case that it is the supervisee who *does the work,* the attentive witnessing and open, curious and encouraging presence of a supervisor is key. This is greatly helped if the supervisor themselves holds an experiential familiarity with such approaches and acknowledges play drives as being key methods to the discovery of self-awareness and supervisory insight.

Little by little and as time passes, I also find myself growing increasingly familiar and secure with the idea of being a supervisor. And so, these recurring encounters with surprise, interruption and emergence seem to be of value as a counterpoint to any complacency and torpor which might otherwise creep into my practice. I challenge myself to remain alert to subliminal elements which might be informing, influencing and shaping the process. To be appreciative of those potentially rich signals from the margins, the sources of which remain just out of view, at the edge, in the long grass, shimmering below the skyline. There but not there. Those subtle communications that strike our senses but perhaps only very rarely grow explicit enough to be written down as an underlined comment on the pages of our supervisory notes.

Alongside all of this, I am with the attendant demands and expectations of the supervisory process. The attempts to discern a line between the concrete and the oblique. Holding and bearing with those worthy and important imperatives I seem to have acquired along the way, to define and deliver a clear outcome for the supervisee. Ideally with some 'next step' practicality with which to equip my supervisee, as they leave my room and venture back to the places and the people with whom they work. It can often seem that the supervisor carries a pressure to always be adding something to their supervisees' process and to always be sending them away with something more, where it might be more helpful to relieve them of something and thereby allow them to return to practice with something less.

In working *with* such tensions, the thoughts of psychoanalyst and supervisor Louis Zinkin strike me as being particularly helpful and sanity supporting;

> What is it that this impossible profession is supervising? Certainly the supervisor, is supervising something, but that something is certainly not the patients' literal analysis. What we call 'supervision' is in reality a shared fantasy – the supervisee trying to imagine what the patient has been doing in analysis and the supervisor trying to do the same. And supervising works best if both are aware that what they are jointly imagining is not true.
>
> (Zinkin, L. 1995: 247)

So as a steadying anchor point when working within these complex and ever shifting interplays, I am here seeking to evolve a method which creates a distilled place for clarification and insight. One that is both open enough to receive a bigger perspective and focused enough to notice and investigate detail. In this I am combining the tangible elements of *walking*, the *choosing* and *placing* of physical objects to mark specific and important aspects of practice and encouragements to be alive to the qualities of embodied and sensory presence that occur along the way.

Multimodality

My working methodology in this enquiry aligns with multimodal approaches, in that the supervisory method itself supports communications and representations which are not limited to the linguistic but also involve aural, gestural, tactile, spatial, visual and embodied modes.

In discussing multimodality and the range of different modes people use to make meaning beyond language, linguists Jeff Bezemer and Carey Jewitt regard multimodality as 'marking a departure from the traditional opposition of "verbal" and "non-verbal" communication which presumes that the verbal is primary' (2018: 183). The MLT method works from a similar premise in that it invites and supports the supervisee to move between and beyond the limitations of such oppositional constructs. In this we see the supervisee making use of several semiotic resources (ibid) in their process of meaning-making. These resources are the very actions and materials the supervisee employs as they work. They include the physical objects and materials being used, the arrangement and layout of the emergent composition, the actions and proxemics involved in the lifting, placing, and viewing of their creative work, and the physical activity employed to achieve the work along with any corresponding auditory commentary. Working in these ways the supervisee is enabled to gain new insights from differing perspectives, both within and without the actual process, thereby developing a richer and multifaceted appreciation of the practice issue being explored. This meaning-making process is characterised by the three key premises of multimodality: '1. Meaning is made with different semiotic resources, each offering distinct potentialities and limitations; 2. Meaning making involves the production of multimodal wholes; 3. (…) we need to attend to all semiotic resources to make a complete whole' (ibid).

In the context of the MLP method, this is underscored by the live and active creative process in which the supervisee is directly involved. This supports further insight which can include an awareness of *those* otherwise overlooked or disregarded aspects of communication. In these ways, a meaningful whole can be established in ways which may be deemed complete. This then, speaks to that apparent supervisory imperative to reach for a complete-enough insight and understanding of that which the supervisee is encountering and experiencing. This in turn, provides for the supervisor, a way to further appreciate and understand what the supervisee is subsequently formulating and seeking to be and/or do.

> Our ability to navigate the multimodality of our work and our art is a crucial key to reaching the deepest layers of our experience as therapeutic companions and artists (…) [to] balance our deepening cognitive concern within the arts therapies with a deepening embodiment of the non-linguistic, boundary-less depths of our practice.
>
> (Porter, 2017: 187)

The MLP method provides both supervisee and supervisor with an expansive framework within which a particular practice issue can be examined both close up and from several distanced perspectives. This offers alternating opportunities for depth enquiry and contextual insight. Through individually identifying and jointly discussing these observations, supervisor and supervisee work together to formulate a clear and shared understanding of the issue to hand.

This then describes something of the role and process of multimodal approaches employed within the MLP method. Next, I would like to outline the containing ritual structure that is used to support and allow for these collaborative and experimental ventures.

The Rites of Passage

In 1909 the Dutch–German–French ethnographer and folklorist Arnold van Gennep produced his best-known and most enduring work in a book entitled *The Rites of Passage* (1960). In this he sets out a three-part schema which codifies an individual's progress as they meet and journey across those thresholds typically encountered through the living of a life. These he describes as *pre-liminality, liminality and post-liminality*. They can also be helpfully understood as being separation, transition and reincorporation.

It is from this schema that I am drawing the basic ritual structure for the method. In discussing his *Rites of Passage* schema, van Gennep drew attention to the need for individual circumstances and emergent needs to be taken into account. This then enables the model to reflect something of specific worth to the experience of the enquirer. In the case of in-training or newly qualified therapists, the method supports them in making sense of and acclimatising to their new and formative roles. Questions might include: *what ways of working need letting go of? What existent skills can usefully be carried across and the identification of supportive and sustaining resources going forwards?* Notwithstanding these considerations, van Gennep also appears to suggest that the need for regeneration (ibid) as an ever-present task in the emergent life of the individual; 'The fact that energy in any system eventually becomes spent and must be renewed at intervals' (ibid: viii). It strikes me that in the practice of this method the supervisee is put in touch with something of the regenerative. The stages of the process prompt and invite this and in the selecting and arranging of the objects, new and hitherto unseen, unthought or unfelt insights may arise. This could be said to occur in all or most creative-based approaches but my sense is that in this method there is a particular alignment between the multimodal and the in-action that can be especially striking. It has been my experience of the method to date that in this regard at the very least, it has proved helpful to supervisees be they in training, recently qualified or seasoned and well experienced in their roles and practice.

The MLP Method Follows a Six-Part Process

1   *Identifying* – the supervisory question
2   *Walking* – establishing and framing the explorative space/connecting with the body
3   *Contextualising* – using materials to represent the practice of the supervisee: past, present and future
4   *Focussing* – using additional materials to mark the specifics of the issue under supervisory consideration
5   *Connecting* – creating an embodied movement sequence
6   *Reflecting* – insights/next steps

1   *Identifying* – the supervisory question

Supervisor and supervisee begin seated in chairs. There is an invitation made by the supervisor to identify and then clarify as necessary, the supervisee's supervisory question. In their book *Creative Supervision Across Modalities*, Chesner and Zografou outline the twofold purpose of identifying and making explicit a supervisory question as being 'an important reflective and reflexive step for the supervisee (...) enter[ing] the role of an active participant' and 'help[ing] the supervisor choose appropriate ways of engaging with the theme' (2014: 28). They also reflect on ways to work with less specified supervisory questions and those which appear more thematically orientated. I have found this method to be able to accommodate both. In the main, I encourage the former and more immediately purposeful approach, whereby the supervisee identifies their key question. I have however also noticed that the MLP process can itself be used as a fertile site within which a nascent supervisory question can emerge and then be clarified and honed.

The MLP method is particularly relevant for supervisory questions and issues that are located or might be usefully considered within a time frame: past, present and future. It is also of use for those instances where a clear way forward seems elusive or challenging. The method reaches into and draws upon the energetic processes inherent within the liminal space and towards the possibility of change. It provides an opportunity to *step back* and view an otherwise consuming situation from varying and potentially clarifying observation points.

Indications and contraindications in considering which approach to take might include the level/experience of the supervisee, their familiarity with creative action methods; thinking and working with metaphor etc; and the strength of the supervisory relationship. On the occasions when I have worked in a more open way, it has been with supervisees well known to me, who have arrived with a live and emergent curiosity to explore a more generalised theme or area of their practice. I have been struck by what they go on to map out as this often links to those transitional, regenerative or relational tropes I mentioned above. Taking these as a cue, I name and invite an explorative and experimental point of embarkation towards the elucidation of the supervisory question as part of a formative clarifying process. Walking is the next step in the process.

2   *Walking* – establishing and framing the explorative space / connecting with the body

Walking is perhaps one of the most immediate, familiar and commonly recognised ways people experience their own body in motion. The notion of the walk is deeply woven into the fabric of our being from the celebrated significance of a baby's first steps to the processional walks which are at the heart of significant ritual ceremonies, marking and underscoring important life events towards and into death.

So the first stage of the method is an invitation to walk. As a supervisor I walk with and alongside my supervisee. As we walk I am pointing out and bringing the supervisee's attention to the space, the path we are making through our walking together. By walking up and down, back and forth we are delineating the space within which the work will occur. This then is the way we identify what might be termed the dramatic space or what theatre director Peter Brook would regard as the *Empty Space*.

I can take any empty space and call it a bare stage. A man walks across this empty space whilst someone else is watching him, and this is all that is needed for an act of theatre to be engaged.

(Brook, 2008:11)

Such a space has been described by dramatherapist David Read Johnson as the playspace; 'an enhanced space where the imagination infuses the ordinary' (1991: 289). Similarly psychoanalyst Donald Winnicott speaks of the *potential space,* an intermediate zone which can be considered a natural site for play (2005: 55). In any case, through our act of noticing and inhabiting it in such ways, it now becomes a live and active space of possibility, that is, a space through which something other might arise. It takes on a liminal quality.

Initially I walk with the supervisee in an entirely unconditioned way. By this I mean I am inviting only the idea to walk, not suggesting or modelling any particular idea of *how* to walk. I track and attune to their rhythm and pacing. Having done so, I invite their self-awareness and consideration around how they are finding themselves walking here, today. There is space here for the supervisee to reflect on this and they may share something of what they notice.

I next talk of ways of walking, I mention the notions of sauntering and meandering. These suggest following a winding course. As a literal act, this may be limited by the realities of the space in which the supervisor practices. The idea in mentioning it here is mainly to encourage connection with the thoughts and feelings which might be conjured by and associated with these particular ways of walking; to be open to other influence, to set aside for now, linear plans or aims. This supports a gradual quality of curiosity, an openness of presence.

I am using no physical elements to mark the boundaries of the emergent space we are now envisaging and occupying together. Nevertheless, it is surprising how clearly delineated it appears. It takes on the quality of a subtle kind of 'walking path' identifiable albeit intangible. It occurs to me that in this, there is a link, albeit unintentional, back to the work of Richard Long whom I mentioned at the beginning of this chapter. To my mind, this part of the method is evocative of one of his earliest works 'A Line Made by Walking' (Long, 1967). In any case, my sense here is that the act of walking itself activates a refined and attuned spatial awareness and a seemingly natural appreciation of supervisor and supervisee in relation to one another, their shared purpose and their co-habited space.

Through walking together, supervisor and supervisee are involved in co-creating and delineating the supervisory space. With their bodies in motion, they embody the supervisory relationship. Importantly, they consciously hold their differing roles, and yet, there is a strong sense of the venture ultimately and essentially being collaborative in nature. Meeting in this way, and at this juncture within the onward evolution of the method, strikes me as being significant. It is in the quality of this intersubjective experience that something is discovered which supports the quality of the onward enquiry. Through the attuned encounter between supervisor and supervisee, a graduated progression of memories, movement motifs, inner sensations and outer observations is welcomed.

I next support the development of this emergent process by introducing some very basic commentary and guidance towards mindful walking. Mindful walking is a practice drawn mainly from the Zen and Vipassana meditation traditions. Here I use one simple element which builds on my earlier invitation for the supervisee to notice how they feel as they walk. I now guide more directly;

> (…) *as you walk, notice and feel the sensation of lifting and placing your feet on the floor, one after the other, as you take each recurring step. To step consciously and to notice this one activity, one step at a time.*
> (Loori, 2007: 97; italics in the original)

Invariably this leads to a slight or apparent slowing down in the pace of the supervisee's momentum and an increased sense of a centered presence in the moment.

These ways of *abiding in* and *reflecting from* the experience of walking, follow in the footsteps of others, from Buddha to Nietzsche. Buddha modelled walking as a practice of non-practice. A way of being in touch with wonders that lie within and without simultaneously. Through taking these observations as objects of meditation, a direct and non-dual experience becomes possible and without the application of apparent or unnecessary effort. Nietzsche spoke of how 'All truly great thoughts are conceived by walking' (Nietzsche, 1889: 10). Recent research continues to examine the links between walking and thinking, especially thinking creatively. In 2014 researchers at Stanford University examined creativity levels of people while they walked versus while they sat. The study claimed that a person's creative output increased by an average of sixty percent when walking. It also seemed to suggest that it was the act of walking itself, and not the environment in which the individual walked, that was the main factor (Oppezzo & Schwartz, 2014).

In thinking about the environment within which this work takes place, it feels important to note that my earliest experiments with this method occurred outdoors. There I noticed that the outdoor environment clearly supported the idea of walking as a natural and easy way into the process. I invited the supervisee to make use of whatever objects the immediate environment offered up, twigs, pebbles, leaves, etc. Subsequently translating and adapting the method to indoor settings required considerations around tone of invitation and how to appropriately calibrate the scope and pacing of the process to the limitations of an interior space. All of this has been entirely possible, and I have since gone on to successfully deliver the work in studio spaces and use it most often in my own relatively small working space. In fact, it is from this space that I have evolved and employed the version of the method that I am describing here.

Once the working space has been delineated by our walking together, I now want to use this quality that the supervisee is connecting with as a way towards the identification or further honing of the supervisory question. At this point, I move away from the supervisee and towards the supervisor's chair. As I move I say, *I'm going to give you a little more time alone to find your natural walking rhythm.* I separate from working in direct and active participation *with* the supervisee to adopt the conscious plain represented by my being seated in a chair. Once seated I observe, aiming to be attentive and available but without appearing overly or intently focused on the supervisee's movement. I now invite the supervisee as they move, to consider what they might wish to bring for supervisory enquiry today. This might be a simple restating of what was previously named. However, I also hold open the notion that as they have been moving in the space, a subtle refinement of the original question may have occurred or that another previously unconsidered question might now be surfacing. I offer time for their reflection, and I wait for them.

3   *Contextualising* – using materials to represent three stages of the supervisee's practice; past, present and future

Once the question has been clarified and agreed, I indicate a selection of materials which I have prepared and set to one side of the main working space. Once, when I ran this method outside in the open air, these were a collection of fallen leaves. Working indoors they are most likely a selection of cloths and small objects. As the supervisee has been describing and refining their supervisory question, I have been listening. Invariably there will have been mention of a before and after (pre and post liminal stage), and an in-between (liminal stage) occurring from the supervisee's narrative account. I ask the supervisee to imagine that which they have described as a 'timeline' comprising three stages; a beginning, a middle and an end. I invite the supervisee to choose and arrange the cloths along this line in a way that marks and represents each of the three distinct sections or stages. In this way a single evolving *path* is made visible in the space (Figure 3.1).

Figure 3.1 The path.

Once the path is composed, I repeat the supervisory question and identify the three parts of the created path as representing the three stages described by van Gennep; pre-liminal, liminal and post-liminal or separation, transition and reincorporation. At this point, I invite the supervisee to describe for me where the essence of their supervisory question might be located within this now visible structure. This most typically occurs in either the pre-liminal or liminal stage. I may choose to dialogue with the supervisee at this point to think and explore options, so as to make the most clear and effective use of the frame being mapped out. I might ask; How might this way of viewing the path be understood in relation to your supervisory question? Responses might include, this is my journey, this is what has happened, and this is my client's process. The task at this point is to formulate the path as being representative of and pertinent to the supervisory question. If the enquiry requires it, I, as supervisor, may take a more directive approach here and suggest the path as being the therapeutic relationship between my supervisee and their client, the process of their work together, the history of their work within this setting, etc.

Figure 3.2 Macro view of the transcribed timeline.

4 *Focusing* – using additional materials to represent the specifics of the issue under supervisory consideration

I direct the supervisee's attention back to the prepared materials and invite them to now select from the various small objects. I ask them to choose objects which can represent specific elements, moments, challenges, feelings and thoughts related to each of the three stages. The supervisee then places these on or in relation to the arranged cloths. Together we now see emerge both a macro view of the transcribed time-line (Figure 3.2) along with the identification of key micro moments within each aspect (Figures 3.3, 3.4 and 3.5).

This integrated and multilayered whole (Figure 3.6) can offer new perspectives and points of connection, parallels and counter-points to support insight, especially towards the formulation of next step consider-ations and subsequent action.

It may be the case that the supervisee naturally begins to share with me the meanings behind the choosing and placing of these various objects. If not, I will ask for something of this to be shared and for them to describe in a sequential order from the pre-liminal, through the liminal and concluding

Figure 3.3 Micro moment 1.

with the post-liminal. Further insights may surface in the telling and as supervisor I will welcome these. I have also learnt to pay particular attention to pacing, sudden gesture, verbal and physical pauses or shifts in movement tone during this episode of the work. Anything that happens and which strikes me in this regard, I will name with interest towards encouraging the supervisee to further connect, acknowledge and identify anything that is surfacing somatically through this stage of the process.

5   *Connecting* – creating an embodied movement sequence
    At this progressed stage of the method there is a sense of the supervisee being in close, perhaps immersive contact with the emergent images and constellations. These may occur in conceptual, aesthetic, sensory or embodied modes. The supervisor may be required to work with some skill to support the supervisee towards a kind of *one foot in, one foot out* orientation to the work. The aim here being to ensure the process remains sufficiently connected with conscious cognitive processing to support a clear and reflective supervisory trajectory, whilst also allowing and following the emergent and intuitive nature of the creative enquiry.

Figure 3.4 Micro moment 2.

Some supervisees will be able to regulate themselves in this regard, others may benefit from additional verbal commentary and/or intermittent dialoguing with the supervisor.

Now the three stages of the path are in place, as represented by the composition of cloths along with key aspects being marked by small objects. The supervisee is next invited to take in the work in its entirety from varying perspectives. I then direct them to return and stand at the beginning (pre-liminal) point of the sequence. This moment further helps to ground and orientate the supervisee in relation to the piece by achieving an overview of the composition as delineating an integrated narrative. The invitation is to now inhabit a still location from which a movement response might begin. This marks a beginning point from which an embodied movement response can be made. In this the supervisee via their embodied self, connects up the stages from pre-liminal through liminality to a final place of completion (stillness) at the concluding (post-liminal) stage.

I invite the supervisee to begin moving into, around, through, across, between the various stages and elements held within the composition. As

Figure 3.5 Micro moment 3.

they do so I suggest they be alive to the general and discrete meanings and associations which have been attributed to the materials used and to very gradually, allow themselves to sense, mark and respond to these meanings within their own body. This may take the form of simply locating their body in relation to a particular aspect, pausing and forming a physical embodied response such as a gesture or an embodied 'sculpt' or evolving an improvised and flowing movement sequence. Some supervisees will be familiar with working with such modalities, others may require more introduction and support to access the process. As supervisor I tend to adopt a role most akin to witness for this part of the process. I am present, there to observe without comment.

Once this stage appears to have been satisfactorily completed I will invite the supervisee to pause and be with the thoughts, feelings and sensations that have been evoked through the process; to be attentive and aware of these. To signal the concluding stage of the process I invite the supervisee to de-role the materials. Once this is completed I direct them back to their chair, thereby returning to the place from where they began. This supports them to now step wholly back into a cognitive and

Figure 3.6 Integrated and multi-layered whole.

conscious domain from which we can together think about the process and what has emerged.

6   *Reflecting* – Insights / next steps

As mentioned above, the process can grow sensorily immersive. In acknowledgement of this fact and to further support a clear transition, I have found it helpful to begin the final reflections by directly inviting the supervisee to take a moment to sit and be back in their chair. This serves to re-emphasise the fact that we are now going to think and reflect on the process together by again recalling the original supervisory question. In this I am reaffirming the link between all that has occurred with the supervisory enquiry. I will repeat their original supervisory question and simply ask, what and in which ways has this process answered the supervisory question? We will discuss and reflect on the points which occur to the supervisee and I may have some further observations from my supervisory witnessing position to offer. Finally I will ask the supervisee to identify next steps which they can now recognise and employ in their practice going forwards.

Further Reflections on the Formulation: The Supervisory Question

In my own work with this method to date, I have found MLP to be especially suitable for supervisory questions which relate to transitions, changes, challenges, blocks or ruptures in the supervisee's therapeutic relationships, professional practice or individual process. These could be regarded as being incidents of liminality, those that are pervaded by a sense of ambiguity or disorientation. The method is particularly helpful in supporting a supervisee reorientate themselves and their thinking following such an incident. Examples might include an instance whereby a supervisee feels lost, adrift or overwhelmed by the process of the work, a therapeutic relationship that is in transition, a long-term piece of work which is plateauing or the effects of institutional change in previously consistent settings. I have also used the method to good effect to support supervisees in building their reflective practice and as a way to scope out where they find themselves in their current career, the choices they have made and the aspirations they hold going forwards. I have used the method with a small group of Level 1 therapists (supervisees) (Stoltenberg, McNeill & Delworth, 1998) to explore anxieties and feeling deskilled in working with the uncertainty and not knowing of therapy. In this example, the method was able to give licence to previously suppressed and disallowed fears. Now instead, it allowed these troubling and difficult to articulate feelings to be shown and crucially, for them to be sited and considered within a bigger picture. They were put in perspective, not just conceptually but via the use of dramatic materials and movement, actually, visibly and sensorily. The breadth and depth of the frame provided a context which was both clarifying and relieving.

Concluding Thoughts

In setting out the method above, I have been taken and further encouraged by the recurring theme of co-creation and the back and forth dialogic encounter between supervisor and supervisee. This seemed to announce itself again and again as I worked to describe the method. As I take this dynamic as being central to the good health and practical effectiveness of the supervisory relationship, I am especially pleased to note and honour its role as seeming integral to the process.

In reflecting on his own work with Daniel Stern, his friend and colleague, Professor Colwyn Trevarthan described their work together as

> a continuous adventure of self-discovery upon the foundations of a dyadic sense of "core self with another" which we communicate in micro-expressive dialogues, never losing continuity of purpose as our objective

and symbolic memories grow and knowledge and skills are enriched in a shared world.

(Trevarthan, 2013: 64–5)

In similar ways, Stern himself appears to have been open to the effect and enrichment from the otherwise unexpected attention of others. In his book *The interpersonal World of the Infant*, he writes of narrative perspectives being applied to non-verbal approaches in ways which honour their integrity whilst enhancing and enriching insight (Stern, 2000: xv).

These strike me as compelling and inspiring reflections to receive in our own roles as creative supervisors and which may in turn further encourage us to explore and experiment with methods such as the one I have attempted to set out here. It is my hope, that in continually exploring the potential for creative and collaborative approaches to supervision, we may grow and expand our own creative and relational fluency in meeting, being with and supporting our supervisees in their practice with others.

References

Bezemer, J. & Jewitt, C. (2018). Multimodal Analysis: Key Issues, in L. Litosselti (Ed) *Research Methods in Linguistics.* London: Bloomsbury. 180–97.

Chesner, A. & Zografou, L. (2014). *Creative Supervision Across Modalities.* London: Jessica Kingsley.

Johnson, D.R. (1991). The Theory and Technique of Transformations in Drama Therapy. *Arts in Psychotherapy*, 18(4): 285–300. DOI: 10.1016/0197-4556(91)90068-L

Keats, John (1899). *The Complete Poetical Works and Letters of John Keats.* Cambridge: Houghton, Mifflin and Company.

Kope, S. Harder, S. & Vaever, M. (2008). Vitality Affects. *International Forum of Psychoanalysis.* 17(3): 169–79. DOI: 10.1080/08037060701650453

Long, R. (1991). *Walking in Circles.* London: Thames and Hudson.

Loori, J.D. (2007). *Teachings of the Earth.* Boston: Shambala.

Nietzsche, F. (1889). *Twilight of the Idols, or How to Philosophise with a Hammer.* Leipzig: Verlag von C. G. Naumann.

Oppezzo, M. & Schwartz, D.L. (2014). Give Your Ideas Some Legs: The Positive Effect of Walking on Creative Thinking. *Journal of Experimental Psychology: Learning, Memory, and Cognition*, 40(4): 1142–52. DOI: 10.1037/a0036577

Perry, C. in Wiener, J., Mizen, R. & Duckham, J. (Eds.) (2003). *Supervising and Being Supervised.* London: Palgrave Macmillan.

Porter, R. (2017). Multimodality, in R. Hougham & B. Jones (Eds.) *Dramatherapy; Reflections and Praxis.* London: Palgrave Macmillan. 169–87.

Stern, D. (2018). *The Interpersonal World of the Infant.* London: Routledge.

Stoltenberg, C. D., McNeill, B., & Delworth, U. (1998). *IDM supervision: An integrated developmental model for supervising counsellors and therapists.* SanFrancisco: Jossey-Bass.

Theoreau, H,D. (2017). *Walking.* Thomastan: Tilbury House.

Trevarthen, C. (2013). Remembering Daniel Stern. *Body, Movement and Dance in Psychotherapy*, 8(1): 64–5. DOI: 10.1080/17432979.2012.756067

van Gennep, A. (1960). *The Rites of Passage*. Chicago: University of Chicago Press.

Winnicott, D. (2005). *Playing and Reality*. Oxon: Routledge.

Zinkin, L. (1995) Supervision the Impossible Profession in P. Kugler (Ed) *Jungian Perspectives on Clinical Supervision*. Einsiedeln: Daimon. 240–7.

Chapter 4

Eco Supervision

Embodied, Embedded, Emergence in Supervision

Therese O'Driscoll

Introduction

Many years ago I moved to Northern Mexico to live and work.

Having recently arrived I was outside a small adobe house washing my clothes on a rock with water I had gathered in the local river. A Raramuri, one of the indigenous people of this region, came and stood outside the fence of the cottage watching my every movement. I had been told this could happen as traditionally the Raramuri are a reserved people who keep distance. Yet, as time passed, I felt my perception of our shared landscape widened by his presence. Somehow sounds, the mountains and the river seemed more present. Two hours later, my clothes by now well washed, this man came over to me and without a word having passed between us, touched my fair hair and said 'cascada de oro', words I later discovered meant waterfall of gold. He then turned and walked away.

The gift of that time was that I had very little Spanish and even if this man had sought to communicate with me through words I would have been unable to do so. The space between us, among the mountains, river and rocks was enlivened with a language not of words but of the ordinariness of daily life – my washing of clothes, his moving presence and openness to the landscape around us and the sound of the waterfall in the river. 'Perhaps not everything can be put into words. (...). [To] receive "*in-formation* via the body can itself stimulate *transformation.*' (Bloom, 2006: 63). The Raramuri are a people of few words. They make statements rather than asking questions. If a question is asked, the first is usually a place-based one such as *where have you come from?* In my experience indigenous place-based cultures are in reciprocity with the surrounding landscape. To paraphrase Abram, the oral tradition of these cultures is based on the belief that everything is alive, has its own speech, rhythm, pattern or song, and there is a call and response to a linguistic world (personal notes, 8 July 2020). The waterfall, brought to awareness by this man's inclusion of it in our dialogue, was deeply honoured and given a place in our meeting.

DOI: 10.4324/9781003034940-5

Eco Supervision – An Emerging Modality

Perhaps, because we had never seen the like of each other before and we were in the spaciousness of unhurried time, this man and I were fresh in each other's eyes. This freshness, I believe, is imperative in supervision. Our work as supervisors is to receive each participant in the supervisory process with fresh eyes and through that process to offer a refreshing, insightful and helpful perspective on what may be happening between the supervisee and their client. Equally to receive the influence of soundscape and landscape, so that the 'other' inherent in that context may also offer perspective to the supervision is important.

Supervision is potentially transformational and is so when 'individuals change their frames of reference; that is the complex web of assumptions, expectations, psychological characteristics, values and beliefs that act as filters through which they view both themselves and the world in which they live' (Holton, 2010: 10). The modality of *Eco Supervision – Embodied, Embedded, Emergence* that I am proposing has developed over time (O'Driscoll, 2015). It is continually emerging and draws on existing theories which can be integrated into well-established models of Supervision. This work is influenced by others in the fields of art, ecology, movement, psychotherapy, eco psychology/ecopsychotherapy and eco spirituality. Specifically my own work and training in Move into Life (Reeve, 2011, 2013, 2021) and Amerta movement practices (Bloom, Galanter & Reeve, 2014) have shaped Eco Supervision considerably. As advocated by these movement practices and by beginning from the place of movement, there is an attitude embodied in the work which 'sees the world as a set of complex, self organizing, adaptive systems (...) where everything mutually *responds* to everything else' (Totton, 2012: 261). I have coined the term Eco Supervision as the prefix eco refers to the inclusion of the ecosystem 'whose elements interact with their surroundings, the ecological, social, intellectual and spiritual context as a unit – the whole house' (Scharmer & Kaufer, 2013: 67). My work includes the places we inhabit and the other than human participants present alongside the human relationships (Figure 4.1).

I situate Eco Supervision primarily within Hawkins and Shohet's Seven Eyed Model of Supervision (2012). I draw on the influences of Dr Jack Finnegan's writings on Bakhtin, dialogics and its application to supervision (2010 & 2013) and Dr Sandra Reeve's work on *the Ecological Body* (2011). This chapter will outline how embodiment, place and emergence incorporated in the supervisory process can offer transformational, creative and dialogic supervision.

The Seven Eyed Model of Supervision

Hawkins and Shohet's Seven Eyed Model of Supervision, devised over 30 years ago, emphasises the relational and systemic which I find helpful.

Figure 4.1 Including the more than human world.

They present seven ways of looking at two interlocking systems, namely the client–supervisee system and the supervisee–supervisor system. The seven eyes are:

> *Eyes 1,2,3* which look at the 'there and then' of the supervisee's work with their client.
>
> *Eyes 4,5,6* which look at the 'here and now' of the supervision session with specific attention to 4, which is the supervisee's process.
>
> *Eye 7* which looks at the context of the work/supervision.
>
> (Hawkins & Shohet, 2012: 86; emphasis added)

Eco Supervision brings an added focus on Eye 7, which 'views the work of supervision as "nested" in increasing wider systemic levels' (ibid: 105). It embraces the view that, 'supervision should not be reduced to the human and material realms, but should also be open to the "more than human world"' (Abrams, 1996 in Hawkins and Shohet, 2012: 110). In practice, most of the supervision I have received has been offered within a room, or online since Covid-19 emerged, with supervisee and supervisor discussing the human-to-human relationships represented. There is little reference or openness to the offerings or attention which the *more than human world* may offer the situation being outlined. Situating the *nesting* in the places where we work seeks to create an ecological consciousness which asks us to engage in 'practices that situate us within a journey, re-entering the world we are acting on and opening ourselves at the deepest levels to learning – the transformation of our fundamental assumptions and beliefs about ourselves and our relationship to the environment' (O'Sullivan, 2004: 2). Eco Supervision situates us in dialogue with our surroundings in a deeply participative way. This idea extends the supervision systems outlined above to include a third system – the environment. This resonates with ecopsychology which can be described as 'the study (logos) of the soul (pyche) in its natural home (ecos)' (Rust, 2020: 51).

Dialogics

Dr Jack Finnegan has written of the Russian philosopher Bakhtin, his work on dialogics and its application to supervision (2010 & 2013). Finnegan describes the work of 'deep transformation' that needs 'a new understanding of language and communication as dialogic, i.e. invested with prior meanings and future possibilities that flow in an interweaving variety of channels; auditory, visual, kinetic, proprioceptive, relational and world impacted' (2013, lecture notes). He outlines five particular characteristics of the dialogic approach to supervision, outlined in italics below. I argue these contribute to the definition of Eco Supervision.

> *'[A] preference for a descriptive poetics'* (ibid). Poetics comes from "poiesis" meaning to make. In Eco Supervision there is a co-creation, a reciprocal making occurring between the human subject of the supervisee and the subjects or natural elements of water, fire, air, wood and earth within which the supervisee is working.
>
> *'[A] preference for a lively passion in the search for transformation'* (ibid). The moving body, in dialogue with the moving body of the earth itself is explored in Eco Supervision. This often generates vitality and a deep sense of being enlivened.
>
> *'[A] preference for a plurality that favours embodiment, coexistence, praxis and dialogue'* (ibid). Eco Supervision is an embodied practice and can be described as poetry in motion. The supervisee shapes their body in the art form of movement in dialogue with their surroundings, in order to articulate the situation they are bringing to supervision.
>
> *'[A] preference for a view that embraces openness, remaining alert to the implications of infinitude and eternity'* (ibid). Non stylised movement imposes no form but rather encourages and supports fluidity, allowing

for an experience of interconnection and interdependence. In the absence of a search for closure or conclusion there is openness to what presences itself to us from the environment. Thus an experience of the numinous may arise in the supervisory process.

'An openness to laughter' (ibid). As supervisees find themselves in communication with the other than human the unexpected often arises and may evoke laughter and deep relaxation.

The Ecological Body

In speaking about supervision Robin Shohet speaks of the importance of the 'what if'. 'That's the purpose of supervision; it's a "respectful interruption" of our work to set up reflective dialogues (...) reflection is the discipline of wondering about (...) what if' (Shohet, 2011: 22).

The articulation we use in supervision is usually the language of words or in the creative approaches, symbols art and metaphors, movement or dance. While speaking is a physical act and therefore embodied, rarely is the whole body engaged in our articulation in supervision. Often we begin from stopping or sitting. What if I were to do something different?

What if I begin from moving and engage with what Dr Sandra Reeve calls *the Ecological Body*? Reeve is a Movement Psychotherapist and creator of *Move into Life* practice. Her doctoral research passes through a historical review of eight ways of seeing the body to arrive at the ninth, the notion of an ecological body. 'The ecological body as a lens takes movement as the basic default, with "stillness" or "stopping" as pauses in the line of movement' (Reeve, 2011: 48). She goes on to describe the Ecological Body 'as a system dancing within systems' with participants engaging with the environment to 'expand their embodied awareness to include the broader context from a position of "being among" rather than "being central to"' (ibid: 50). What then if I work in a way in supervision that situates us in the world we are embedded within and gives value not only to our human relationships but also to the natural world within which we abide?

Key Identifiers of Eco Supervision

What might identify Eco Supervision as a modality of supervision? What might we do differently if we depart from the traditional way of doing supervision and give time for the connection between supervisee, supervisor *and* environment. I propose three core identifiers, each one contributing to the whole.

Embodied

In Eco Supervision there is the openness to work with the articulation of the whole body through movement rather than from the articulation of words only. In order to prepare for this it is necessary for supervisor and supervisee to engage in a dialogue which allows them to give time to this different articulation. Each begins from movement and pays attention to their own embodied presence. Drawing from Move into Life and Amerta movement practices, I offer the guidance of receiving our own condition, receiving place and receiving other. This moves both parties away from seeking, grasping or a more cognitive approach to supervision. It opens each person to an embodied dialogue with ourselves (receiving our own condition), and it prepares our ecological sensitivity to the place we are in (receiving place) and enables us to be in communication with each other (receiving other) through movement. The opening of our sensitivity to others in place *before* tuning in to the human other is important. Crucially it situates the human-to-human relationship within the materiality and presence of time and place. Thus, we begin by weaving our own bodily matter with the matter we are situated within and from here spread awareness to the human-to-human relationships.

This is a dynamic approach that looks not just at gesture or position but at the whole dynamic of mind, body, feeling and spirit – all in movement. It is like the difference between taking a photograph and a video clip of someone. One represents a moment in time, a snapshot of be-ing; the other represents a series of moments, a process, a be-coming in time. Eco Supervision engages the whole body of both supervisee and supervisor to investigate 'how to make one's own three-dimensional bodily experience more conscious as a container for receiving the transference, projective identification, and counter-transference more fully' (Bloom, 2006: 39). Our bodies become a very valuable tool to receive and listen to what is going on in supervision and become the feeling, sensing, intuiting, and seeing *eyes* as outlined in the Seven Eyed Model.

Embedded

Supervision is about generating fresh perspectives on the material brought to supervision 'or at least the possibility of a new response to the familiar perspective' (Chesner & Zografou, 2014: 18). If we take this seriously, we must also evaluate supervision differently. It is not problem-solving but rather a reflection on the question: *did the supervision offer any fresh perspectives?* Working actively with the context within which supervision is held, be that an indoor or an outdoor place, enables us to work with perspective in a creative and imaginative way. Our relationship with place is very important. 'There is power in place, in the environs we find ourselves and how they impact who we are and how we respond' (Rust, 2012: 62). Eco Supervision includes place not as a backdrop to the human-to-human relationship but as an active participant in the supervisory relationship. 'The world is sensing us while we are sensing it. It is not a passive recipient of our attention but a deeply reciprocal partner' (Robertson 2012:269). This widens the container of supervision to include the faces and voices of many others aside from the supervisor,

Figure 4.2 Subjects in a reciprocal relationship.

allowing fresh perspectives to be offered to the work. The rock, tree, orna-
ment or stream become subjects, not objects, in a reciprocal relationship
(Figure 4.2).

Emergence

Gardening is a way to practice emergence, transformative learning and creativity. Sometimes in spite of all our plans, the garden has other seeds, weeds
and plans to reveal its own organic nature. Eco Supervision works with emergence and is not unlike gardening. The supervisee chooses where to work
and spends time there, open to what the soil or the place may offer or reveal.
This being-present-to-context, to what is real is a right brain hemisphere
activity that 'alone can bring us something other than what we already know'
(Mc Gilchrist, 2009: 40). Staying with this process can be difficult. It is an
openness to stay with the not-yet known therefore uncertain, until the new
arises. It is 'a letting go to let come' (Scharmer & Kaufer, 2013: 29). This
approach is consistent with what some writers in supervision describe as *the
not knowing stance* (Shohet, 2008). In what may come or be revealed, it is
potentially transformative.

Eco Supervision in Practice

In Eco Supervision I attend to my supervisee by first moving alongside them in the way I outlined above. Movement is a right hemisphere of the brain activity that makes connections and sees things from the whole. This is important for 'the nature of right hemisphere attention means that what-ever we experience comes to us first – it "presences" to us in unpreconceived freshness – in the right hemisphere' (McGilchrist, 2019: 17). This 'presences' to us provides a strong link to Finnegan's favouring of dialogics and poetics, and Reeve's openness to the influence of the environment.

We work within the landscape of my garden and cabin studio, 'a meeting place of human, nature and spirit' (Jones, 201: 161). I move with and witness the supervisee as they select the place they wish to work and we both receive the witnessing of our environment.

This practice of witnessing is well known to those engaged in Authentic Movement practices: 'the ground form is a practice between a mover and a witness' (Goldhahn, 2007: 23), which simplified into its most basic form is a non-directed movement where one person moves with their eyes closed and the other witnesses, offering 'acceptance and goodwill' (ibid). In Move into Life and Amerta movement, movers move mainly with eyes open and witnessing is widened to include receiving the influence of the envir-onment where 'we practice tuning with each other and with the situation' (Suryodarmo, 2014: 311).

This openness to receiving and becoming aware of all that is around us while being received by earth, wind, flower, stream or place is pivotal in Eco Supervision. This is the supervisee–supervisor–environment triadic system in motion. An example of this is while pushing against a stone I receive the yielding of the earth beneath me. At the same time, I notice my supervisee pushing against the earth while receiving the support of a tree at her back.

Case Study

In the case study below Una is the supervisee, her client in therapy is Mary and 'I' am the supervisor.[1] Excerpts of Una's own account of the supervision are in italics.

In this supervision session, Una wishes to focus on her client Mary whom she has seen on a number of occasions. Una experiences Mary as very with-drawn. She feels distant and notices it is difficult to make contact with Mary. As Una has described feeling very free when working outdoors and feels resourced by nature we agree to work with this client through movement and in the garden. *The intention in supervision was for me to be able to get a better understanding of what it is like to be my client so I can bring back questions to our sessions that may help me to move closer to her. I felt the need to understand her situation more fully.*

I invite Una to articulate through her own body how this client presents in her body, her gestures, her posture, her way of walking, as well as verbal and non-verbal descriptions of her issues and symptoms. Una walks around the garden with her head bowed, heavy in her walking, somewhat crouched over. Finally, she settles with her back to a large rock in front of which is long grass recently strimmed. I suggest she embody Mary's condition and the heart of the issues and questions she is bringing to therapy. *I was aware of the sense of needing to hide and not be seen. Finding a rock that hid me from behind felt good but there was still a sense of being seen.*

Una reaches out and picks up a large swathe of grass and covers her head (Figure 4.3). *When I put the old cut grass on my head and I was covered in dry grass I became aware of how shallow my breathing was. I was aware of my eyes closed and being in my own world.*

As a supervisor I am an involved witness in this unfolding dynamic. I am aware of Una's movement and the movement around us in the garden, of air, water and bird flight. I notice I want to shrink back and wonder if I am too close to her. In the light of Una's description of struggling to get close to this client, I wonder how my own felt experience may relate to her client's process. For now I pause. When Una sits and places the grass on her head,

Figure 4.3 Embodied, embedded, emergent.

I am deeply moved. When there is no further sound or movement from Una, I notice sound appears louder to me in the garden, such as the birds chirping and water in the stream flowing. Una appears to not notice. I choose to draw out what is happening in her body using Gendlin's *Focusing techniques* (1981).

> *My supervisor then asks me to describe the sensations I am feeling and the emotional quality I am experiencing. It is clearly anxiety. In time she invites me to say hello to that anxiety. When I do, this enables me to open my eyes, my breathing becomes deeper and I connect with a red flower, the only thing I can see clearly through the dry grass. I am aware that there are other things around me but I cannot, nor do I want to, connect with them all. Somehow, because this is all I can see, I can connect with it. This red flower has no expectations of me, no need for me to do anything, it simply is and allows me to be. I feel seen in my uniqueness as I see it in its uniqueness.*

With time, it is clear Una has come to a resolution of her work. She is still, yet there is a vitality in her stillness and she appears, in contrast to earlier, alert to her surroundings. Her breathing is deep and she seems very relaxed. I invite her to close her movement. She slowly removes the grass from her head, rises to stand and turns to touch the rock which had been supporting her back with her hand. Finally she turns again to incline her head in the direction of the flower. I suggest she wipe down her body as if to remove Mary's story from her own. This is an important gesture of differentiation between her own self and her embodiment of Mary's experience before we speak. When the session is over, I will do the same to let go of my own experience in witnessing.

Subsequent Reflection

Time is needed for digestion and assimilation after exchanges such as this and once the movement is complete my supervisee and I come together to process what has happened. Sometimes this happens through the spoken word, other times through drawing and painting.

As a supervisor and witness in this digestion-assimilation, I offer back to my supervisee two main felt experiences. One is the felt experience of shrinking and the fear of being too close to Una in the garden space. This we felt was a parallel process to what Una had experienced with Mary as her client (eye 5 of the Seven Eyed model) as well as what Mary experiences with her husband. The second is of noticing sound in the environment as Una became quieter having sat at the rock. Birds were singing, declaring their place in this shared landscape yet Una appeared in deep withdrawal. In electing to ask her to speak, to name her felt sensations, I sought to invite her voice into the dialogue around her. This invitation enabled her to speak *and* to open her eyes. This three-dimensional felt experience – rock at her back, grass on her head, followed by eyes opened and seeing the flower to her front – enables her to understand Mary's dilemma further. *I get the sense of her withdrawing from the world and yet her need to be seen as her own unique self.* This moment of being witnessed by an animate, sentient other who is not human, afforded a very felt experience of her client's wish to be seen while at the same time wanting to hide. Had her eyes remained closed, Una may not have experienced this simultaneous difference.

'It is not just for us to be aware of the world. The world wants to look in' (Robertson, 2012: 269). The experience of the red flower presenting itself to Una, looking in as it were, meant she decided to change her approach to her therapeutic relationship with Mary. She describes offering more witnessing in their relationship. *I offered choice and no expectations of what my client should or should not do. We explored in the therapeutic relationship how it was to be witnessed and heard by me as the 'one' in the room. I found over time my client was able to describe feeling able to make contact with me sometimes and other times withdrawing. Yet more and more she noticed the difference and the transition between the two. We worked with how her relationship is with her partner and how touch is so hard for her and equally how her relationship with her mother is now. We have spent some time exploring what happens to her when I see and hear her as she describes this in the therapeutic setting.*

In addition, Una noted she is now inclined to listen and observe Mary more from the starting place of movement rather than from stopping. *I noticed the increase in the length of Mary's sentences, the flow in both her body and conversation and the lightness in her step as she left the room.* This bodily recognition of the difference in the movement of conversation, difference in mood and walking steps is very helpful as the work progresses with clients and supervisees. Finally Una shares in supervision sessions how this process of Eco Supervision offers her an alternative perspective on what may be happening with other clients. She describes how this process enables her, when meeting her clients, to articulate her questions more concretely and to explore the in-between space more accurately.

Conclusion

I began this chapter speaking of a transformational experience for me of being witnessed over time by a Raramuri. His presence opened my perception of the landscape we shared and heightened my awareness of the sound and voice of the waterfall. To develop our 'being as indigenous' is to be deeply in relationship with place and 'to grow the circle of healing to include all Creation' (Kimmerar, 2013: 211). Eco Supervision seeks to grow this circle of healing so that our work is nested in the wider systemic field of place.

Eco Supervision is an invitation to slow down. It seeks to alter our habitual mode of attention of starting from stopping or stillness and instead beginning from movement. By being in the changing which movement implies, it offers a felt experience of flux and the influence of not only the human-to-human relationships which are embedded in that place but also all the other relationships present. Eco Supervision recognises that among other sentient beings many faces and voices can be added to the container, dialogue and field of resonance of supervision. We are always in relationship and the 'I' is held within a wider 'We'. It gives value to working creatively, giving time and space to be with the unknown so that new perspectives or enlivened realisations can dawn in the supervisory and client–supervisee relationships.

The case study outlined how the relationship with a rock, a swathe of dried grass and a red flower offered fresh perspectives to the supervision process and allowed for the felt experience of simultaneous difference between a hiding and a wishing to be seen. This offered the supervisee a deeper understanding of what was happening with her client and enabled her to adapt her therapeutic approach accordingly.

Much has changed in the world in which we are nested as I write this chapter. Covid-19 has meant virtual gatherings have become a lot more common. Supervision may be face to face but at the time of writing rarely held in the same room. Bloom's question 'how to makes one's three dimensional bodily experience more conscious as a container (…)?' (2006: 39) has never been more relevant as we seek to find our volume and three-dimensionality while facing little boxes on a flat-screen. The multiple intelligences of naturalistic, auditory and proprioceptive knowings can easily be flattened in the face of this dominance of the visual field.

I suggest that the practice of movement engages us as participants in the change which is all around us and can be the home ground of potential transformation. Movement may be practised online, across time and space, as well as in a shared place. Perhaps more than ever we are invited to develop our ecological consciousness, situate ourselves within a journey and reflect on the world we are acting upon. Our relationship to the living matter within which we live requires our attention. Eco Supervision offers an opportunity for embodied development of this consciousness.

Acknowledgements

The author wishes to acknowledge with gratitude her supervisee Una for her agreement to contribute the case study for this chapter and for sharing her own ongoing research into this modality of Eco Supervision.

Note

1   Not real names.

References

Abram, D. (2011). *Becoming Animal.* New York: Vintage Books.

Abram, D. (2020). The Ecology of Perception [Podcast interview]. *Emergence Magazine.* 20 July 2020. Available at https://emergencemagazine.org/story/the-ecology-of-perception/

Benefiel, M. & Holton, G. (Eds.) (2010). *The Soul of Supervision.* New York: Morehouse Publishing.

Bloom, K. (2006). *The Embodied Self.* London UK: Karnac Books.

Bloom, K., Galanter, M. & Reeve, S. (Eds.) (2014). *Embodied Lives.* Axminster, UK: Triarchy Press.

Chesner, A. & Zografou, L. (2014). *Creative Supervision across Modalities.* London: Jessica Kingsley.

Eichhorn, N. (2012). Ecopsychology. An Interview with Mary-Jayne Rust. *Somatic Psychotherapy Today* 1(4): 62–4.

Finnegan, J. (2010). Dialogue and Theory in Clinical Supervision. In M. Benefiel & G. Holton (Eds.) *The Soul of Supervision.* New York: Morehouse Publishing. 120–51.

Finnegan, J. (2013). Faces and Voices [Lecture notes]. 8 October 2013. All Hallows College, Dublin.

Gendlin, E. (1981). *Focusing.* New York: Bantham.

Goldhahn, E. (2007). 'Shared Habitats: The MoverWitness Paradigm'. PhD thesis. University of Plymouth.

Hawkins, P. & Shohet, R. (2012). *Supervision in the Helping Professions* (4th edn). Milton Keynes, England: Open University Press.

Jones, T. (2014). The Musical Portal. In K. Bloom, M. Galanter & S. Reeve (Eds.) *Embodied Lives.* Axminster: Triarchy Press. 157–64.

Kimmerar, R.W. (2013). *Braiding Sweetgrass.* Canada: Milkweed.

McGilchrist, I. (2009). *The Master and his Emissary.* New Haven & London: Yale University Press.

McGilchrist, I. (2019). *Ways of Attending.* London & New York: Routledge.

Oliver, M. (1992). *New and Selected Poems.* Boston: Beacon Press.

O'Driscoll, T. (2015). Eco Supervision; Toward an Ecological Consciousness in Supervision. *Inside Out* 77(Autumn): 41–51.

O'Sullivan, E. & Taylor, M. (2004). *Learning towards an Ecological Consciousness. Selected Transformative Practices.* USA: Palgrave Macmillan.

Reeve, S. (2011). *Nine Ways of Seeing a Body.* Axminster: Triarchy Press.

Reeve, S. (2013). *Body and Performance.* Axminster: Triarchy Press.

Reeve, S. (2021) *Body and Awareness.* Axminster: Triarchy Press.

Robertson, C. (2012). Dangerous margins: recovering the stem cells of the psyche. In Rust, M.J. & Totton, N. (Eds.) *Vital Signs.* London: Karnac. 265–78

Rust, M.J. (2020). *Towards an Ecopsychotherapy.* London: Karnac.

Rust, M.J. & Totton, N. (Eds.) (2012). *Vital Signs.* London: Karnac.

Scharmer, O. & Kaufer, K. (2013). *Leading from the Emerging Future: From Ego-System to Eco-System Economies.* San Francisco: Barrett-Koehler.

Shohet, R. (Ed.) (2008). *Passionate Supervision.* London: Jessica Kingsley Publishers.

Shohet, R. (2011). *Supervision as Transformation.* London: Jessica Kingsley.

Suryodarmo, S. (2014). Interviews with Prapto, Solo, August 2013. In K. Bloom, M. Galanter & S. Reeve (Eds.) *Embodied Lives.* Axminster: Triarchy Press. 306–17.

Totton, N. (2012). "Nothing's Out of Order": towards an ecological therapy. In M.J. Rust & N. Totton, N. (Eds.) *Vital Signs.* London: Karnac. 253–64.

Chapter 5

The 'Four Chair Method'

An Integrative Approach to Creative Supervision

Hannah Sherbersky and Martin Gill

Introduction

As psychotherapists, we span three interconnected practice traditions, psychodrama, dramatherapy and systemic family therapy. These disciplines are no strangers to embodiment and the sensory world, and in our own respective professional roles, we explore the embodied experience of supervision, how a client and situation has moved us, or a story touched our hearts. We are interested in the dialogical-reflective activity of supervision; the exploration and exchange of perceiving, thinking and talking 'from within' the complexity of an ongoing situation and what this looks and feels like (Shotter, 2010: 37). The originator of psychodrama, J.L. Moreno, believed that physical, social and psychological expression enabled a whole person 'insight integration' (Moreno, 1953) sometimes occurring in a cathartic way and bringing symptom relief. The role of the psychodrama therapist is to trust the body's communication as part of this process. Dramatherapy, rooted in early child development theory, shares an understanding of the complex psycho-social importance of embodied sensory experience in attachment and brain development (Jennings, 2011). The child's capacity to be curious, exploring meaning through movement, drama, sounds and expressive metaphors with others, is seen as a natural human developmental trait that can be revisited during adulthood to bring insight, acceptance and new meaning and symptom relief for a range of problems.

We both understand supervision as a creative collaboration between supervisee and supervisor, tasked ultimately with upholding our professional therapeutic practice. As supervisors, we are striving for relational responsivity, being fully present within the relationship (Afuape, 2017) and focusing on the moment-to-moment processes that enable an embodied experience in which the supervisor and supervisee can utilise insight through action (Sherbersky & Gill, 2020).

As embodied therapists, we are reminded that our bodies exist in social and professional contexts (Afuape, 2017). I (HS) am a white British woman of South African and Jewish parentage, and my family arrived here in the 1970s

DOI: 10.4324/9781003034940-6

seeking political asylum from the apartheid regime. I am a systemic family psychotherapist, with a background in mental health nursing and now work as a clinician, academic and researcher at the University of Exeter. I (MG) am a white British man, working as a psychodramatist and a dramatherapist in private practice and often work with couples and families, drawing on systemic ideas to inform my practice. As an arts therapist, my relationship to an embodiment and an externalisation of feelings is a measured one, where I've learned how 'less' is sometimes 'more' when working with less extraverted individuals.

In this chapter, we describe an action-based supervision exercise, the Four Chair Method, developed from our integrative supervision practice of family therapy, psychodrama and dramatherapy. The Four Chairs is a playful model that draws on a structured and spontaneous approach, inviting the more expressive and performative aspects of supervision, without the need for the term that often instils dread in a group of trainees: 'role-play'. It is used primarily with groups but can also be adapted within individual supervision (Sherbersky & Gill, 2020). The exercise was influenced and inspired by a dramatherapy supervision exercise, the *Four Elements* created by Zografou (2013: 49) and the systemic intervention of *Internalised-other Interviewing* (Tomm, 1989).

Here, we present two case studies of the model and show how an understanding of aesthetic distance and role theory help to inform this approach. The origins of our modalities stem from shared systemic roots and philosophical principles (Chesner & Zografou, 2014; Sherbersky & Gill, 2013, 2020). In our ongoing working relationship, we have shared a mutual respect for each other's approach and have often devised training workshops and group work for colleagues and trainee supervisors as part of NHS services and family therapy training.

The supervision ideas and techniques described in this chapter were developed and formed over several years, born out of a sense of innovation and curiosity about the points of intersection and divergence between our models. We offer joint training provisions to a wide range of mental health service clinicians and supervisors, and participants come from a range of modalities where there was a commitment to reflect on supervisory practice and to add new skills. There was also an expressed desire to give a boost and refresh practice that had become formulaic and repetitive.

At the time of our early workshops in 2010, a shared understanding of action-based clinical supervision practice and its underlying standards and philosophy was largely an unexplored and under-theorised area. Evidence-based verbal practice approaches, then as now, were influencing NHS trust procurement decisions and the prospect of integrating robust supervision competencies with creative action approaches was relatively novel.

Our focus in training has been on how supervision can, without losing rigour and professional therapeutic boundaries, become a creative process between the supervisees and supervisor (Patel, 2004). Through incorporating action methods and describing their clinical value and fit, we offer supervisors a new bank of resources that can be integrated to enhance their practice. The Four Chairs Method is a synthesis of several of these techniques. In our clinical experience, many supervisors work creatively in their own clinical settings, but lose confidence and vitality in developing an action approach in the supervisory process. At times, participants suggest that they saw only arts therapists and psychodramatists as distinct creativity specialists and working creatively in this way had not been part of their own therapy training. As a result, they had steered away from these techniques.

A key component of the Four Chairs is an invitation to be spontaneous. Spontaneity and creativity in action are fundamental to psychodrama, and although conceptualised less centrally, is not new to family therapy. Over 40 years ago, Gregory Bateson, an anthropologist and social scientist and commonly regarded as a grandparent of family therapy, suggested our goal in therapy is an informed spontaneity (Bateson, 1972). Bateson also reminded us that all relational feedback is indeed a process of spontaneous learning; 'the shape of what happened between you and me yesterday carries over to the shape of how we respond to each other today' (1979: 24).

To help our groups conceptualise and validate the clinical application of action methods, we offer several key principles when working in action including therapeutic spontaneity (Bateson, 1972); psychodramatic role-theory (Moreno & Bridges, 1944); action insight (Kellerman, 1992); physical and aesthetic distancing and proximity techniques (Moreno, 1966) and a systemic framework (Bateson, 1956; Minuchin, 1974; Carr, 2014). From these key ideas, we then introduce and rehearse a series of psychodramatic exercises such as doubling, role reversal and mirroring that can be utilised in the systemic supervisory context (Sherbersky & Gill, 2020).

Systemic Roots

A systemic perspective emphasises that individuals need to be understood within their own ecological and visceral context (Bateson, 1972). Individuals, families, groups and organisations can all be seen as self-regulating systems, in which the behaviour of each person/s mutually affects and is affected by the behaviour of others – which applies equally to the supervisor/supervisee relationship. The behaviour within this relational context furthermore has a communicational value, the meaning of which can be understood only within that particular context and emphasising the multiplicity of meanings (Sherbersky, 2020). Linear causality is replaced with circular causality, as each different part of the system interacts with others in recursive loops of communication. 'Symptoms' within any given system may be understood to be potentially providing stability, and furthermore, the 'problem or symptom' can potentially then be maintained by repeated unsuccessful attempts to solve it in the same way (Watzlawick, Weakland & Fisch, 1974). Active embodiment then enriches multiple perspectives or discoveries from within the system.

Systemic theory and practice bring important insight to the world of embodied supervision; as systemic practitioners, we actively work to engage families and supervisees alike in a reflexive inquiry about the systems in which we all function. Within the field of systemic theory and practice, we understand systemic reflexivity to mean attending to 'a conscious cognitive process whereby knowledge and theory are applied to make sense of remembered reflective episodes' (Dallos & Stedmon, 2009: 3). The clinician and supervisor attend to and recognise how their own experiences, personal resonance and stance influence and contribute to the therapeutic engagement with clients, and to the supervisee. The clinician's subjective perceptions of their own interpersonal power and inequality are important aspects both of personal reflective and reflexive processes within supervision (Dallos & Stedmon, 2009).

By helping the supervisors to move their supervisees into action, we suggest that they can begin to think and act 'on their feet' trusting their gut and creative spontaneity. At other moments, depending on the material being explored, we introduce cognitive insight distancing techniques, such as physically stepping back or forwards, perhaps using small-world objects to promote aesthetic distance (Sherbersky & Gill, 2020).

We anchor the work in systemic ideas that support spontaneous thinking in the supervisory context and illustrate how closely the psychodrama model fits within a systemic approach. Deacon (2000) for example, in an exploration of divergent thinking within supervision, describes the four subparts of the divergent thinking process; fluency, flexibility, originality, and elaboration and asserts that therapists, of all theoretical orientations, are drawing on divergent thinking skills, perhaps without realising.

Aesthetic Distance and Use of Space

Arts therapies in general privilege the use of emotional and psychological distance techniques (Jennings, 1998), for example, using masks, movement or metaphors and 'indirectly, seeking to achieve a protective balance away from overwhelming emotions and cognitive processes (Landy, 1983). In contrast, psychodrama uses a more action-analytical approach (Kellerman, 1992), inviting meaning and action to come together within a considered and supported reparative clinical framework. The use of the mirror (seeing oneself through another's eyes) role reversal (embodying another perspective) and double (coming alongside) techniques described here, can be considered to represent somatic, cognitive and social domains (Moreno & Bridges, 1944).

Edward Bullough first coined the term aesthetic distance in 1912, although it had been in existence from the days of the first cave paintings. It refers to the gap between a viewer's conscious reality and the fictional reality presented in a work of art (Cupchik, 2002). Artistic appreciation according to Bullough is obtained by;

> Separating the object and its appeal from one's own self, by putting it out of gear with practical needs and ends. Thereby the 'contemplation' of the object becomes alone possible.
>
> (Bullough, 1912: 87)

The term distance here refers to the capacity to step far away from a work of art and then to come closer and in some cases to step inside and become part of a sculpture or video, for example. Supervision, like therapy, provides a space to step back, allowing us to reconstruct and reshape our understanding of our patients' spoken and unspoken needs and contemplate their meaning. These reflexive aesthetic positions are not new to systemic theory. Lang, Little and Cronin (1990) described how an 'aesthetic domain of action' serves as a creative bridge between 'production' and 'meaning': 'Systemic theory argues that our professional practice requires constant creative elaborations and radical reconstructions' (Lang, Little & Cronin, 1990: 7).

Burnham and Newns (2013) encourage supervisees not to attach to their theories too rigidly, stating that within therapy there can also be an over-emphasis on problems. Sometimes families say things have improved prior to their first appointment, but this is not always what the therapist wants to hear (Burnham and Newns, 2013). They argue how the client's own existent creative solutions, curiosity, and optimism and resilience need to be prioritised. Action and spontaneity training can form the basis of this process.

Spontaneity – Thinking Fast and Slow

Our innate capacity to interpret events and either work on impulse or carefully think things through in a structured way is part of the evolutionary survival mechanism that helped our ancestors to know when to keep still, run or fight from threats (Kahneman, 2011). Kahneman makes a distinction between fast intuitive and slow cognitive thinking in a modern context and suggests that an awareness of these two mechanisms can help us to explain why some people have 'high cognitive ease' with their environment, whilst others suffer from cognitive dissonance or low cognitive ease' around many aspects of daily living; politics, personal self-doubt to climate change and disease control (Kahneman, 1982).

Many impulse disorders such as conduct disorder and behavioural addictions are characterised by more extreme variants of fast thinking modes. Medication and talking therapies often invite sufferers to slow down and create structures to help them to manage these impulses.

In our supervision workshops, prior to moving into action, we describe a distinction between therapeutic spontaneity and impulsivity (Sherbersky

& Gill, 2013). Rather than negating the benefits of embodied spontaneity and fast thinking, we invite an environment and structure of appropriate quick humour, immediate thinking, body reactions and quick-witted lateral-thinking. Within psychodrama, the need for an adequate physical and emotional group 'warm-up' is an essential prerequisite (Holmes & Karp, 1991). We often start a training program with a playful game or group warm-up, asking people to stand and map where they have travelled from in relation to others or say their name and make a body gesture that expresses their mood.

Working in pairs or small groups, we then invite participants to embody feelings or thoughts they may be bringing to supervision. We invite these small groups to share a visual image through mime or embodiment. In addition to preparing the group to work in action, the group warm-up can also be seen as a warm-up for the facilitator, helping to identify shared themes or struggling individuals. For us, the term embodiment is also a relational experience, not only confined to our skin-bound somatic self, but the ways in which these embodied experiences change when we are engaging with a calm therapist or active group member in a safe, reflective space. We are embodied, but also boundaried, denied and located by others (Hardham, 1996). Shotter (2008) also describes how spontaneous new behaviours, thoughts and actions can arise, not only from our own centre of experience but have their locus in a relational, interactive context. In the following method, participants experience the invitation to attune to the instinctive wisdom of embodiment and spontaneity in the role as a natural experience, one which opens up the shared experience of therapeutic complexity in a vivid and helpful way.

Four Chairs Method

This particular exercise evolved in supervision groups with trainee family therapists, drawing on original ideas from two different modality sources: a supervisory dramatherapy exercise, the Four Elements created by Zografou (2013: 49), and the systemic intervention of 'Internalised-other Interviewing' whereby individuals are interviewed as the internalised other, i.e. in role (Tomm, 1989). The exercise is particularly useful when managing complexity in supervision by breaking down specific ideas and aspects of the supervisory question. It utilises action insight, whilst exploring and experimenting with roles, and emphasises one of the central principles of systemic practice; the notion of multiple perspectives (Sherbersky & Gill, 2020). The supervisor has the flexibility to attune to the level of expressive creativity and confidence of the group and or group members; for supervisees who may be more inhibited and less used to working in this way, roles may be chosen that are more concrete and cognitive. For other groups, more challenging and demonstrative roles may emerge. In both instances, the exercise can uncover unconscious and intuitive responses to the work. Over time, experienced supervisors will learn how to adapt the exercise to suit the group. Maintaining the roles, the structure and the 'stage' all become important to provide containment during the exercise.

Group Method:

Set out the chairs in a room in the following way (see Figure 5.1):

1. The supervisor sets out the chairs as below. Setting the scene and dividing the space between the 'audience' and the 'stage' is important. Notice the group's potential collective response to the sight of empty chairs; the anticipation of this supervision exercise as an event can cue the supervisees into action. They may also need reassurance and explanation as the supervisor sets up the space.
2. One supervisee from the supervision group is invited to bring a supervisory question or dilemma and sit in the supervisee's chair. They are invited to talk to the supervisor (who is sitting in the supervisor chair) for 5–10 minutes to explore a supervisory question. The group sit opposite the chairs, much like an audience. They listen as the supervisor discusses the case and then establishes with the supervisee which chairs they would like to utilise. The supervisor prompts and suggests ideas, for example: 'would you like to hear from the identified client, their parent, or someone from the clinical team?'. Chairs 3 and 4 always remain the same in any exercise; 'outrageous possibilities!' and 'next steps' as shown in Figure 5.2.
3. The supervisor then invites group members to come and take on the roles in the chairs. The names of each role or position can be written on paper and placed in front of each chair as an aide-memoire. The group members are encouraged to embody their role, noting how to sit and where their attention is drawn in their bodies. The supervisor might also summarise what they have heard from the supervisee.
4. The supervisor then interviews each role, inviting a spontaneous 'fast thinking' response. Whilst this is happening, the supervisee is encouraged

Figure 5.1 Four chairs method for supervision – set-up.

Figure 5.2 Four chairs method for supervision.

to just listen and perhaps take notes. This is an opportunity for the supervisee to reflect. The group members in the chairs (roles 1 to 4) do not talk directly to the supervisee or each other. Note that the supervisee's chair is turned away from the other chairs to support this process. The supervisor must hold the space firmly, and direct and prompt where necessary. If a general discussion were to ensue between the different roles and or between supervisee and the roles, the supervisee would no longer be able to take a 'meta' or mirror position, and the exercise could quickly become muddled and confusing.

5.   The supervisor maintains their position in their chair and interviews each role in turn, drawing out new ideas that relate to the supervisory question. When appropriate, other members of the larger groups can then volunteer to role reverse or 'double' the feelings, gestures and thoughts of each perspective. They indicate to the supervisor their wish to double and come and stand alongside the relevant chair, expressing unspoken or insightful feelings or thoughts that they have observed from their audience position. Whatever chairs are used, the exercise always includes the penultimate chair as 'outrageous possibilities' – which offers the supervisees permission to be truly spontaneous and creative, using irreverence and exaggeration. This is finally followed by the 'grounded' chair: the 'next steps'. This role talks from their own clinical experience and offers ideas about what could happen next.

6.   The final part of the exercise rests back with supervisee and supervisor, discussing what they have heard and providing the supervisee with an opportunity to reflect and integrate their own ideas.

7.   All group members are then thanked and invited to de-role and sit back with the larger group. At this point, all group members talk not about the content of the supervisory material but any personal resonances and reflections they have experienced during the exercise. The supervisor invites those who took on roles to offer any insights from their experience, but is careful that they do not go back into role. The exercise is then complete.

Figure 5.3 Multiple possibilities using numerous positions or chairs.

Depending on time and clinical expediency, additional chairs can be included to those identified by the supervisee and can include client, family member/s, or any other part of the wider system: social worker, therapist, care worker, neighbour and friend. Importantly, it can also include an abstract and externalised aspect of the work; the 'symptom', ethics, professional competency, the theories, the 'not yet known', and so on (see Figure 5.3).

Supervisees who use this action method describe it as providing a reassuring structure from which many creative ideas can emerge. Complex aspects of the work can be broken down and expertise held within the group can be drawn out. Furthermore, group members can be invited to experiment with the role that they find harder to understand or empathise with.

Clinical Example: Group Supervision with Rachel

I keep people in their place and maintain the status quo!

In a monthly supervision group, Rachel, a trainee family therapist and recently qualified psychologist, was working on placement within a learning disability team. In a group session using the Four Chairs, she presents a complex clinical dilemma. Despite her trainee status, she feels she had been placed in an inappropriately expert position within her team. Her placement supervisor, with the support of the multidisciplinary team, had suggested she offer her insight and solutions regarding a learning disabled client, Eddie, who was being aggressive and violent towards the support workers who cared for him during handovers. She had been asked to offer reflective sessions to these support workers and found that few attended and she felt demoralised and de-skilled.

Rachel in the initial supervisory discussion, describes feeling anxious about the expectations placed on her by the team. She is invited to describe the context and her position within the team and the client. The supervisor explores Rachel's feelings about her relationship with her multidisciplinary team members (MDT) and her 'felt self' regarding Eddie. Her supervisory question focuses on how she could be both more effective, but also feel more confident and authoritative in her position. Rachel and the supervisor discuss which roles will be invited in the chairs and agree on the following; the client, the support workers, the multidisciplinary team (MDT), the 'aggression', outrageous possibilities and next steps.

Group members volunteer to take on these roles and sit for a few moments of quiet, while they 'get into' their roles. They are encouraged to sit in a way that represents their role, and the supervisor invites them to be thoughtful about their embodied experience. The supervisor then interviews each person in role in turn, noting her own embodied response and drawing on her own curiosity and intuitive line of questioning. Each role speaks for a few minutes about their (imagined) ideas about the situation, including Rachel's role with the team. As each role 'talks', a few from the rest of the group who were seated as the 'audience,' volunteer spontaneously to step up and double the role, extending and deepening the reflection. The final conversation takes place between the supervisor and Rachel, and she talks through her surprises and resonances, when hearing the multiple perspectives from the chairs. What transpires is a powerful and informative narrative about parallel processes between Eddie, his support workers and Rachel. Key themes and words that are spoken in role are described in the table below:

Chair 1 Client. Eddie	Chair 2 The support workers	Chair 3 The 'Aggression'	Chair 4 The MDT	Chair 5 Outrageous Possibilities	Chair 6 The Next Steps
I Just want some control	No one understands what we put up with	I feel powerful!	We don't understand why this aggression and violence is happening	Eddie and Rachel need to devise the care package without any other involvement	I suggest Rachel meets with her supervisor to share the experience of this group supervision
I don't know or care about that person called Rachel	Rachel is new inexperienced – we would rather meet with her supervisor	I keep people in their place and maintain the status quo	We have put everything in place that is needed	Eddie doesn't really need any support anyway. He should be discharged	Rachel needs to engage with the support workers in a different way – can she find out what they want?

(continued)

Chair 1 Client. Eddie	Chair 2 The support workers	Chair 3 The 'Aggression'	Chair 4 The MDT	Chair 5 Outrageous Possibilities	Chair 6 The Next Steps
I have no choice about anything in my life, so at handover, I get angry with the staff. It makes me feel powerful	We don't get to choose who supports us	I keep people on their toes	We keep offering support but it is rejected and we are too busy to keep attending to this issue	The support workers must be forced to attend the reflective practice group – or their pay is docked	Can Rachel share reflections on this parallel process with the team?

Through the group's embodied and imagined reflections, a gradual, considered, 'slow thinking' narrative emerges that helps Rachel recognise the parallel process around power and control – with her, Eddie, the support workers and even the MDT reporting a sense of powerlessness. The surprising and spontaneous position of 'outrageous possibilities' offers, (as is always the case) a nugget of gold for the supervisee. In this instance, an amplification of how little control Eddie or the support workers have, and the mismatch between what the MDT believed they were doing, and the experiences in the team. Rachel is given an opportunity to reflect, using the aesthetic distance in the model to see that she had inadvertently been set up without any real sense of agency. She had authority afforded to her by her supervisor, but it was not recognised by the people she was trying to support, and she therefore had the illusion of authority with no power. The supervisor and Rachel talk about power, gender, her trainee status, as well as her own feelings of self-doubt. She is able to see more clearly where and how she needs to intervene, and how a systemic understanding of the whole scenario brought a more compassionate understanding of Eddie, the support workers and indeed her own position.

Clinical Example: Using the Four Chair Method in Individual Supervision With Kevin

Being a full partner

Individual supervision can utilise this exercise by inviting the supervisee to role reverse themselves with each role in turn. They swap between their own chair and the roles they have identified. In all other respects, the exercise remains the same, with attention given to maintaining clarity between roles and thoroughly de-rolling between each chair. If space is an issue, cushions can be used and the exercise can even be marked out using small world objects (Chesner, 2008). The following case example illustrates how the model can be adapted to work with an individual supervisee.

> Kevin, a locum GP, is struggling with a commitment to either retire early to join his already retired partner John, or to stay with the practice and increase his hours. The supervisor invites Kevin to draw four chairs on a piece of paper (or the online whiteboard), and to label each of these as follows: 1 "The problem" 2. Kevin's partner; 3 Outrageous Possibilities; 4 Next steps.
>
> The supervisor then invites Kevin to describe the problem in more detail and asks him to imagine sitting in the chair and speaking as if he is the problem. In role, Kevin expands on the meaning and impact of leaving work or leaving John to lone retirement. It becomes clear that there are two components to the leaving chair, to leave or stay. So Kevin is invited to draw a fifth chair: the leaving chair. Kevin is then encouraged to make statements in support of each of these divergent positions. "I don't have a full pension to live off, I will be financially dependent on John", "I'm afraid", "I will miss my patients", "I'm unhappy that I am not a full partner in the practice", etc.
>
> Managing the available time constraints, the supervisor then invites Kevin to imagine sitting in the outrageous possibility chair and invites him to think quickly in an uncensored way about solutions to his dilemma. Kevin laughs and says: "I could ask John to go back to work and stop pressuring me". "I could buy John a cat or a dog", "I could leave both chairs and go travelling for a year!" "We could adopt a child!".
>
> In the 'next steps' chair Kevin reflects on the earlier explorations and is able to consider a forward-moving position to manage the conflicting feelings and impulses he has been experiencing. In a final reflective conversation, away from the chair positions, the supervisor validates Kevin's next step decision to set a future point in time where he and his partner John can discuss a timeframe for planning retirement together and what they can do meanwhile to enjoy their differences.

Considerations

Our individual practices have benefitted significantly from our integrative explorations into the modalities of systemic and psychodrama practice, and our supervision maintains a pace that allows participants to do as little or as much as they feel comfortable with. We are often impressed by the levels of engagement and sense of freedom participants report about their participation and being offered permission to tap into their creativity and spontaneity in a structured way. When supervisees are invited to explore personal resonance and experience using aesthetic distance and action techniques, we should not underestimate the heightened level of affect that can sometimes be activated, and therefore, the manifestations of power need to be explored (Patel, 2004).

In all supervisory relationships, the context of power held by the facilitator is important. Within an action-orientated space, aspects of diversity and privilege hold added significance, requiring insight, experience and sensitivity in how these techniques and methods are introduced. In group supervision, group members can sometimes be overzealous in their enactment and present powerful dramatisation of a colleague's work, so thorough de-rolling and sharing at the end of a supervision session is particularly important.

Supervisors using the Four Chair method need to attend to the group process, whilst focusing on the pace of the supervisee. We encourage supervisors to try a gradual integration of action-based ways of working into their supervisory practice and to attend at least one group led by a skilled practitioner or trainer. The development of psychodramatic skills and techniques, like those of family therapy, are learned most effectively through experience of both being a student and a participant in therapy and training. In our ongoing integrative practice using systemic and action-based models, we continue to remain respectful of each other's differences and similarities. By doing so, we keep our individual and mutual practice curious, innovative and safe.

Concluding Thoughts

The Four Chairs method and other creative approaches, discovered through the convergence of our distinct practices, have enabled us to develop new embodied structures and frameworks where grounded clinical ideas can be explored alongside a more spontaneous approach. We use this exercise in a variety of settings – both in face-to-face sessions but increasingly now online. As therapy practice has developed digitally, clinical supervision online has also had to innovate. Supervision and therapy models have to be considerate of the multiple contextual shifts with which practitioners are contending, and the shift in the 2020–21 digital context as a result of the pandemic was complex for student, supervisor, clients and families alike (Sherbersky, Ziminski & Pote, 2021). One of the biggest challenges when supervising online is the need to create a sense of presence (Lehman & Conceição, 2010). The Four Chairs method can be adapted to be used in digital supervision, with the option of changing names on the screen and inviting those who are observing the session to turn their cameras off while spotlighting others. Consideration needs to be given to the 'interplay between feelings, thoughts and behaviours online, the physical world in which the student is situated and their private inner world of imagination and experience' (Sherbersky, Ziminski & Pote, 2021: 6). This consideration and invitation to notice the embodied experience of this exercise can enhance a sense of online presence.

The Four Chair structure, adapted for use in live group, individual or in online forums, enables our supervisees to find new solutions to complex or entrenched problems and supervisors to revitalise their practice. The 'outrageous possibilities chair' makes it permissible to present embryonic, innovative and creative ideas in a tangible and contained way, leading to insight and possibilities for change. We encourage supervisors and supervisees to try this exercise and enjoy![1]

Note

1   All case material and clinical examples are drawn from composite cases to preserve confidentiality.

References

Afuape, T. (2017). Supervision as a relational responsivity. In J. Bownas & G. Fredman (Eds). *Working with Embodiment in Supervision.* Routledge: London. 89–104.

Bateson, G., Jackson, D., Haley, J. & Weakland, J.H. (1956). Towards a theory of schizophrenia. *Behavioural Science*, 1: 251–64.

Bateson, G. (1972). *Steps to Ecology of Mind.* New York: Ballantine.

Bateson, G. (1979). *Mind and Nature: A Necessary Unity.* London: E.P. Dutton.

Bullough, E. (1912). 'Psychical distance' as a factor in art and as an aesthetic principle. *British Journal of Psychology*, 5: 87–117.

Burnham, J. & Newns, K. (2013). "I'll be the coat hook and you be the mother". Improvisation, Action & Drama in systemic practice. *Context*, 126: 3–6.

Carr, A. (2014). The evidence base for family therapy and systemic interventions for child-focused problems. *Journal of Family Therapy*, 36: 107–57. DOI.org/10.1111/1467-6427.1203236: 107-157

Chesner, A. (2008). A passion for action and non-action. In R. Shohet (Ed). *Passionate Supervision.* London: Jessica Kingsley. 132–48.

Chesner, A., & Zografou, L. (2014). Philosophical and theoretical underpinnings. In A. Chesner. & L. Zografou (Eds.) *Creative Supervision across Modalities.* London: Jessica Kingsley. 17–41.

Chimera, C. (2013). Getting our mojo workin' – the magic of action-methods therapy through a neuroscience looking glass. *Context*, 126: 24–6.

Cupchik, G. (2002). The evolution of psychical distance as an aesthetic concept. *Journal of Culture and Psychology*, 8(2): 155–87. DOI.10.1177/1354067X02008002437

Dallos, R., & Stedman, J. (2009). Flying over the swampy lowlands: Reflective and reflexive Practice. In R. Dallos & J. Stedman (Eds.) *Reflective Practice in Psychotherapy and Counselling.* Maidenhead: Open University Press. 1–22.

Deacon, S. (2000). Using divergent thinking exercises within supervision to enhance therapist creativity. *Journal of Family Psychotherapy*, 11(2): 67–73. DOI.10.1300/J085v11n02_06

Friedlander, M. (2012). Therapist responsiveness mirrored in supervisor responsiveness. *The Clinical Supervisor*, 31(1): 103–19. DOI.10.1080/07325223.2012.675199

Hardham, V. (1996). Embedded and embodied in the therapeutic relation-ship: understanding the therapist's use of self systemically. In C. Flaskas and A. Perlesz (Eds). *The Therapeutic Relationship in Systemic Therapy*. London: Karnac. 71–89.

Holmes, P., & Karp, M. (1991). *Psychodrama: Inspiration and Technique*. London, New York: Routledge.

Jennings, S. (1988). Dramatherapy and groups. In S. Jennings (Ed.). *Dramatherapy. Theory and Practice 1*. London, New York: Routledge. 1–18.

Jennings, S. (1998). *Introduction to Dramatherapy*. Philadelphia: Jessica Kingsley.

Jennings, S. (2011). *Healthy Attachments and Neuro Dramatic Play*. Philadelphia: Jessica Kingsley.

Jennings, S. (2020). Dr Sue Jennings and EPR. Retrieved (2021, December 16) from www.suejennings.com/epr.html

Kahneman, D. (2011). *Thinking, Fast and Slow*. New York: Farrar, Straus and Giroux.

Kahneman, D., Slovic, P., & Tversky, A. (1982). *Judgment under Uncertainty: Heuristics and Biases*. New York: Cambridge University Press.

Kellerman, P. (1992). Action Insight. In P. Kellerman. *Focus on Psychodrama*. London and Philadelphia: Jessica Kingsley. 85–95.

Kellerman, P.F. & Hudgins, M.K. (2000). *Psychodrama with Trauma Survivors: Acting Out Your Pain*. London and Philadelphia: Jessica Kingsley.

Ladany, N., Friedlander, M.L., & Nelson, M.L. (2005). *Critical Events in Psychotherapy Supervision: An Interpersonal Approach*. Washington, DC: American Psychological Association.

Landy, R. (1983). The use of distancing in drama therapy. *The Arts in Psychotherapy*, 1(3): 175–85. DOI.org/10.1016/0197-4556(83)90006-0

Lang, P., Little, M., & Cronen, V. (1990). The systemic professional: domains of action and the question of neutrality. *Human Systems* 1(1): 34–49.

Lehman, R. & S. Conceição, Initial. (2010). *Creating a Sense of Presence in Online Teaching: How to "Be There" for Distance Learners*. San Francisco: Wiley. 21–4.

Leyland, M.L. (1988). An introduction to some of the ideas of Humberto Maturana. *Journal of Family Therapy*, 10(4): 357–74. DOI.org/10.1046/j..1988.00323.x

Minuchin, S. (1974). *Families and Family Therapy*. London: Tavistock Publications.

Minuchin, S., & Fishman, H.C. (1981). *Family Therapy Techniques*. Harvard: Harvard College.

Moreno, J.L. (1946). *Psychodrama. Volume 1*. City: Beacon House.

Moreno, J.L. (1953). *Who Shall Survive? Foundations of Sociometry, Group Psychotherapy, and Sociodrama*. New York: Beacon House.

Moreno, J.L., & Bridges, F. (1944). *Spontaneity Theory of Child Development*. New York: Beacon House.

Moreno J.L. (1966). The Creativity Theory of Personality. *Spontaneity, Creativity and Human Potentialities*. University Bulletin of Arts and Sciences. 66(4): 19–24.

Moreno, Jonathan. (1994). *Psychodrama since Moreno*. In P. Holmes, M. Karp, & M. Watson (Eds). London: Routledge.

Patel, N. (2004). Difference and power in supervision: the case of culture and racism. In I. Fleming and L. Steen (Eds). *Supervision and Clinical Psychology: Theory, Practice and Perspectives*. Sussex: Brunner-Routledge. 108–35.

Sexton, T.L. & van Dam, A.E. (2010). Creativity within the Structure: Clinical Expertise and Evidence-based Treatments. *Journal of Contemporary Psychotherapy*, 40(3): 175–80. DOI.org/10.1007/s10879-010-9144-2

Sherbersky, H. (2013). Integrating creative approaches within family therapy supervision. In A, Chesner & L, Zografou (Eds). *Creative Supervision across Modalities*. London: Jessica Kingsley. 89–108.

Sherbersky, H., & Gill, M. (2013). Rediscovering spontaneity. *Context*, 126: 34–8.

Sherbersky, H., & Gill, M. (2020). Creative action techniques in supervision, *Journal of Family Psychotherapy*, 31(3–4): 79–95. DOI.org/10.1080/08975353.2020.1802175

Sherbersky, H., Ziminski, J. & Pote, H. (2021). The journey towards digital systemic competence: thoughts on training, supervision and competence evaluation. *Journal of Family Therapy*, 43: 351–71. DOI.org/10.1111/1467-6427.12328

Shotter, J. (2010). Movements of feeling and moments of judgement: towards an ontological social constructionism. *International Journal of Action Research*, 6(1): 16–42. DOI.10.1688/1861-9916_IJAR_2010_01

Shotter, J. (2013). Agentive spaces, the "background", and other not well articulated influences in shaping our lives. *Journal for the Theory of Social Behaviour*, 43(2): 133–54. DOI.org/10.1111/jtsb.12006

Shotter, J. (2008). *Chagrin Falls*. Ohio: Taos Institute Publications.

Shklovsky, V. (1917). Art as Technique. Retrieved (2021, December 16) from https://muratgermen.files.wordpress.com/2009/11/viktor-shklovsky-art-as-technique.pdf

Tomm, K. (1989). Externalizing the problem and internalizing personal agency. *Journal of Strategic and Systemic Therapies*, 8(1): 54–9.

Van Der Kolk, B. (2014). *The Body Keeps the Score: Brain, Mind, and Body in the Healing of Trauma*. New York: Viking.

Watzlawick, P., Weakland, J.H. & Fisch, R. (1974). *Change: Principles of Problem Formation and Problem Resolution*. New York: W. W. Norton.

Yalom, I. & Leszcz, M. (2005). *The Theory and Practice of Group Psychotherapy* (5th edn.). New York: IUP.

Zografou, L. (2014). Four elements: groups supervision and playback theatre. In A. Chesner & L. Zografou (Eds.) *Creative Supervision across Modalities*. London: Jessica Kingsley. 59–70.

Chapter 6

Mirroring Within Supervision

Julie Joseph

The influence and impact of movement on our bodies have been a subject of writings for centuries. Bergson in offering 'I see plainly how external images influence the image that I call my body: they transmit movement to it. And I also see how this body influences external images; it gives back movement to them' (Bergson, 1911: 18) continues this dialogue. In this chapter, I offer an addition to the existing conversations, exploring the use of movement in my supervision practice.

At the time of writing this chapter, the world is facing significant challenges: from a pandemic and climate change to campaigns such as Black Lives Matter. A sense of shifting, adapting and managing change is very present within our communities as well as in our private and professional lives; this demands a raising of our conscious awareness.

Supervision, which plays an important role in the wellbeing of our staff and clients, particularly in these times, requires a level of adaptation too. How we as supervisors connect, support and deliver supervision is undergoing a shift in focus as many of the familiar ways of working need to be reorganised and renegotiated. More and more supervisors are supervising through computer screens and not meeting in person. As a consequence, we require to attend to new ways of accessing the non-verbal, the physical connections and the energetic threads. The lack of having the physical bodies of the supervisee and supervisor together in a room, as well as supervisors noticing the impact of this on their own minds and bodies, prompted an interest in focusing on the role of the body in the work we do.

When the pandemic hit the UK and lockdown was first imposed in March 2020, I began by noticing: 'what, within all of this change, was I called to?', 'What was certain within me and around me?', 'What could I rely on and what supported me as a supervisor in this unfamiliar time?' I returned home to my body and to the practice of the Discipline of Authentic Movement (DAM), 'a mystical practice centered in the development of embodied witness consciousness' (Adler, 2021: page number). This practice, which involves a shift of attention from our presence in the external world to a focus on our internal landscape, offers a direct route to the wisdom of the body. The practice is

DOI: 10.4324/9781003034940-7

based on the development of a mover-and-witness relationship and our own inner witness (Pallaro, 1999: 257). It offers some interesting parallels with the supervisory space, the supervisory relationship and access to inner wisdom. Supervisees, in accessing their own insight, are often in touch with their feelings and emotions which they access through their body, and they are in touch with a wisdom that comes from within themselves (is internal). And just as the supervisor holds an awareness of the growth of the relationship between them and their supervisee, they will also hold an awareness of the development of the supervisee. Witnessing them moving from perhaps a place of reliance or dependence on their supervisor to being more professionally confident and with only conditional dependency on the supervisor (Hawkins & Shohet, 2012: 70).

Sitting at a computer screen and holding an awareness of the skills I was using within this online supervisory space, as well as of how I was adapting my skills to this new way of working, was the beginning of what became the basis of my research and ultimately the offering in this chapter.

During sessions when I am using my body's felt sense and my skills as a witness, I noticed that mirroring had become a dominant concept and showed up time and time again.

Within Dance Movement Psychotherapy (DMP) mirroring or reflecting is a well-known and well-used concept. The therapist mirrors or reflects back, via their own muscular activity and verbal narration, what they perceive and experience in the body action and the body of the client (Levy, 2005). Mirroring also involves kinaesthetic empathy (Meekums, 2012; Rova, 2017), an embodied way of sharing empathic reflection. Mirroring may also be envisaged as a therapeutic movement relationship. Clearly distinct from mimicking, mirroring involves accessing the meaning of movement, not simply copying the action of the other. In DMP, mirroring is used with individuals and groups in a range of ways.

However, in supervision it seems to be a less explored concept. Those who write about mirroring (Hawkins and Shohet, 2012; Farnsworth, 2010; Paintner and Beckman, 2010; Moore, 2016) often relate it to verbal mirroring, when the supervisor repeats the words or phrases of the supervisee. Although Payne (2008) does use it in her supervision practice in the form that Dance Movement Psychotherapists would recognise, she is writing mainly for DMP professionals. Farnsworth (2010) discusses mirroring as a way of supporting the person to see themselves as they really are and as a way of creating a more fluid psyche in supervision. But again, he discusses it when used verbally or in writing. Moore (2016) discusses the role of mirror neurons and burnout, compassion fatigue and secondary trauma, particularly among those in the helping professions. He offers reflexive supervision as a way of exploring and making meaning of the emotional narrative. Paintner and Beckman (2010) offer a range of examples of movement and dance exercises to bring to supervision, where the body is recognised as carrying wisdom; however, they do not explore the specifics of mirroring and how one might recognise and use this specific technique more fully.

Currently mirroring is receiving renewed attention from professionals and researchers due to discoveries in neuroscience of neurons dubbed 'mirror neurons' (Jeannerod et al., 1995; Rizzolatti & Arbib, 1998; Gallese, 2001). They are named mirror neurons because they fire both when observing and when performing actions. Mirror neurons are activated in response to the motor movement of another: they fire in an identical pattern to that of the one who moves (Cozolino, 2014). In other words, corresponding sensori-motor networks in our brain are activated when we observe another person in action. The discovery of the neurons in the frontal cortices of our brain, where networks converge to process high-level information, sheds light on how we communicate. Positioned in this area, as if at a strategic crossroads of inner and outer experiences, they enable us to begin to understand how we communicate without words. Some have hypothesised that mirror neurons were vital to the evolution of language by creating social interactions which were based on sharing an object, for example. This evolved into hand gestures and then into symbolic language (Arbib, 2002).

The discovery of mirror neurons offers new insights into the functional architecture of consciousness, allowing us to consider and explore the mechanisms by which both conscious and unconscious material is processed and activated. The function of mirror neurons offers the most comprehensive picture yet of some physiological reasons why mirroring can be an effective way of engaging supervisees in the supervision process.

Using Hawkins and Shohet's seven-eyed model, I explored when and where mirroring is clearly present, useful and evident. The seven eyes are:

1. Focusing on the client and how they present
2. Exploration of the interventions and strategies used by the therapist/supervisee
3. Focusing on the relationship between client and therapist/supervisee
4. Focusing on the therapist/supervisee
5. Focusing on the supervisory relationship
6. The supervisor focusing on their own process
7. Focusing on the wider context in which the work happens

(Hawkins and Shohet, 2012: 80)

In my supervision work, I noticed that the concept of mirroring showed up most frequently when working with the relationship between client and therapist/supervisee (eye 3), the therapist/supervisee themselves (eye 4) and when focusing on my own process as supervisor (eye 6).

I suggest that mirroring and therefore the conscious use of mirror neurons can play a part in creating a safe environment, as it supports attunement and helps to build empathic responses. Arguably, mirroring can also play a role in accessing insights and wisdom within the body, whether in individual or group supervision. The mirroring of the other's gestures, postures and movement, as well as their verbal expressions, is an intervention which can be used with supervisees whether or not they are familiar with movement-based practice.

For many years I have worked with young people who have significant histories of trauma and abuse and with the staff who support them. Much of my work has been dedicated to dealing with the impact of abuse on these young people, the vicarious trauma experienced by the staff who support them and the effects of all of this on organisational culture. The body of someone who has suffered abuse is often well defended, which can result in that person rejecting anything that risks breaching those defences. Most of the young people I work with are also adolescents whose natural pull at this stage in life, is towards learning from their peers rather than from adults. They are moving towards independence, so 'being seen' by an adult professional can be problematic for their emerging identity, as it makes them feel more self-conscious. The combination of these complexities enables us to see how practitioners may encounter many hurdles, particularly when using embodied interventions with adolescents. Within my organisation it also became apparent that vicarious trauma can impact all members of the organisation: care staff, administration staff, leaders and other stakeholders. Interested in attending to the well-being of all staff and stakeholders, I searched for an approach to supervision that would be holistic, flexible and accessible. It is through the process of developing this approach that I recognised the importance of mirror neurons.

Different Ways of Using Mirroring in Supervision

Embodied Presence

I will often share with supervisees my awareness of my own physical body – how it feels, how it is positioned and where I hold any tension – as well as sharing my inner landscape, my feelings and emotions, where they are and how they feel and move in me. It is important that I ensure that my experiences are located in the present moment and are therefore relevant to the session and what might be between us or simply around us. I use this sharing as a way of using my own embodied presence as a mirror for the other (the supervisee). It is a way to invite them to reflect on their own personal experience and to support their enquiry becoming more about their embodied experience and less about their thought process. In this way I offer a metaphoric mirror. Because the experiences I share originate within me, often my supervisee will feel separate enough from their own internal world that they feel safe from unwanted exposure. However, their mirror neurons are still active, so the supervisee is accessing information without having to dive too deeply into the unknown realms of their own bodies. It is a gentle and supportive way to introduce the 'unknown', the information their bodies hold. Supervisees often report feeling closely accompanied by me as a supervisor – with my mirror neurons ensuring that I am in a close relationship with them. My shared awareness comes from a place that we create between us, as well as from within me.

Reflecting During My Own Supervision Sessions

Reflecting on my own experiences with my supervisor and with peers during peer supervision sessions, I explored the potential use of mirroring in different areas of the supervision session. Questions that arose in these contexts have supported this deepened exploration of the use of mirroring. They include: *Is mirroring accessible to all supervisors regardless of their training and background?*, *How do 'non-movers' tap into this tool?*, *Where does mirroring show up in the supervisory space and is it useful for supervisees?* and *What is the shadow of working with this concept in supervision?*

Mirroring and Preparing for the Session

In this first of five vignettes mirroring is experienced in the space just before the session. I call this *pre-transference mirroring*, where my body is already responding to what I consider an energetic action from the other as we prepare to meet. I am curious as to whether I am responding to a memory in my own body or to something new that is arising. Kathleen (as I call her here) is a supervisee who prefers to reflect through moving. Her supervision follows a routine where, as supervisor, I prepare for these sessions by creating space within myself. As I orient towards our time together, I bring my attention inwards and become aware of what I am carrying emotionally, physically and energetically. This awareness acts as a catalyst for shifting, moving and clearing out in order to be more spaciously present for the work ahead and to make room or space for whatever arises in the session. Taking my attention to my felt sense and body knowing (Gendlin, 1981: 10), I prepare to witness Kathleen. Below, I describe how I understand this part of the work as *pre-transference mirroring* (Paterson, 2020).

> As I prepare to meet Kathleen I feel something in my body. Sitting waiting for her to arrive on Zoom I notice a heaviness within; a slow, rather sluggish sense in my limbs and a thought: 'I can't be bothered'. I am curious as this is unexpected and does not match how I have been feeling up until that moment; I make a note of these sensations and this thought. My supervisee arrives on screen and after a moment's pause says: 'I'm overwhelmed and can't be bothered'. We explore how she knows this. She reports a heaviness in her body, a tiredness and a wish to rest. Supervision then continues with a restorative focus, giving space to explore tensions in her body and finding

ways to release them. We explore and acknowledge the complexities of the context within which she works, physically moving around the room and finding physical objects to represent each of the complexities and placing them in relation to herself. We then take time to notice and wonder about her direct experience of each object and her somatic resonance with it. Finally, as we prepare to end the session, we focus on grounding her within this working context. Helping her find her physical presence, weight and stability within her own body.

Mirroring and the Environment

Mirroring is an integral aspect of the role of the supervisor when attending to the creation of a safe supervisory alliance. In an earlier paper, I discussed how empathic reflection, which includes mirroring, is essential in establishing a safe holding environment. Indeed, without this sense of safety, it is difficult to access what is hidden within us which includes our insights; instead, our attention is taken up with maintaining defences from the potential threat of the relationship or environment (Joseph, 2017: 209). When the experienced embodied supervisor mirrors the supervisee's quality of movement, the supervisee may experience a sense of being 'met' and accepted. This reaches far greater and deeper layers of existence than what the spoken word can touch. By sharing a breath rhythm and attuning to the tension and flow in the muscles and to the movement of the other, adjusting our shape and the space between us to empathetically meet the other we begin to build trust (Homann, 2017: 45). Through this embodied form of mirroring, we attune and create safety. Bloom (2006) suggests that mirroring helps with insecurities in the relationship – an important consideration with new supervisees, including those completely new to supervision. Because of the shared physicality of the experience with each other, the supervisee feels seen and welcomed exactly as they are. This rapport through mirroring yields a deep sense of acceptance.

Mirroring and Hospitality

My way of holding and creating a hospitable space has been changed by the impact of working online during the pandemic. The importance of visual information when other senses, such as sound are distorted or even completely absent as is the case for smell and touch, has heightened my awareness of what is supporting my ability to sense the other. In this second vignette, I offer an example of how I used mirroring to support the arrival and settling of my supervisee, whom I call Beth.

We are working via video conferencing. Beth arrives exactly on time. I am struck by the speed of her speech and by how she is constantly moving even when seated. Clothes are being rearranged, her hands pick at threads, her

Figure 6.1 Mirroring and hospitality.

head moves quickly from side to side. Our eyes do not meet. There is such a sense of distraction and I become aware of the unsettledness this brings into my body. I mirror this back to her and comment on how restless she seems. I share with her how witnessing her feels in my body, with my heart speeding up and my stomach constricting. I tell her how the muscles in my face feel held in a tight mask and my shoulders feel tense, as if I am ready for flight, prepared to run and react quickly to anything. I explain that I feel exhausted already. At this point our eyes meet (see Figure 6.1). She stops and pays attention to what is happening within herself. After having reflected back to her what I noticed from a deeply attuned place, I take a deep breath and slowly exhale; I drop my shoulders and gently hold her gaze. I relax into my chair and pause. The intention is to offer Beth my active body for her to observe and model consciously or unconsciously. Using my knowledge of the mirror neuron pathways, without words this time, I offer the possibility of a change in the quality of her physical presence. It is as if I say 'here I am, here you are. I see you, I am with you, I am like you. You are welcome'.

Mirroring When Supervising in Groups

Meekums (1992) discusses the use of mirroring or reflection in group work. She describes how it can be useful if the group loses its way and needs a level of leadership. She suggests that mirroring offers this support by creating a group experience, limiting the potential for splitting or disintegration

Figure 6.2 Mirroring when supervising in groups.

of the whole group into separate individuals (as in Figure 6.2). By sharing an action, collaboration is ignited between all members of the group. The shared movement leads and holds this part of the work. In group settings the mirroring, reflecting and witnessing of others also offers an opportunity for insight to arise through the movement of others. This can be a subtle change where we are 'seeing things differently' (Meekums, 2006: 173). In the context of supervision, mirroring in movement could therefore be a way for the supervisee to notice themselves by reflecting on the other. This third vignette is an example of my practice of group supervision where even those who do not choose to take part in the sharing of movement are affected as a result of mirror neurons.

Today I am supervising a group of trainee supervisors using my embodied approach. I can tell that they are anxious and unsure, so I begin by giving them permission to sit out if they do not want to be actively engaged. The only stipulation I have is that they don't leave the video conference room, our virtual shared space and that they stay and observe the process. I am confident that they will still be able to resonate with the group, knowing that their mirror neurons will be firing. Fraser, a male practitioner, opts to sit out, to be on the video call but not to take part. The individuals in the group take turns in offering a movement or gesture which the others copy. A story begins to emerge. This becomes the topic for supervision. The group proceeds to working with the movements they have offered, eventually choosing one gesture that resonates with them all. This gesture is mirrored by the whole group until it develops into a new gesture with an associated meaning. By the end of the supervision session, all in the group are able to reflect on their insights as individuals and on what resonated with them. I notice that Fraser, who had initially chosen not to take part in the embodied process, joins in with this discussion. He explains that this option had offered him the opportunity to be part of the group process but on the edge of it. He reports: 'I felt as if I was still part of this group, following the movements, feeling very present'. I notice that the group accepts this as if he had phys-ically moved with them. His insights are accepted as part of the story. He too has been to group supervision and has engaged in a meaningful way with the embodied process.

Mirroring and Insight

Moving together within the supervisory relationship is another way of witnessing the other (Figure 6.3). When there is good enough holding and the supervisee is able to be seen (witnessed by the other), insights may arise (Joseph, 2017). A pause, an emotional shift and sense of confusion in the supervisee often, marks a moment of insight. In a similar way to how it happens in a therapeutic relationship, when the supervisor has attended to hospitality and created a safe container of the supervisory space, it becomes possible to access insight or wisdom (Winnicott, 1965: 47; Slochower, 1996).

Sometimes I physically mirror the movement of my supervisee, in an abbreviated way, in order to experience their movement within me. I then offer my words as a reflection to support their conscious awareness. Alternatively, tapping into my DAM practice, I may consider my supervisee as a mover, and from this perspective, I am their witness. In this role, I sit, do not move, but instead sense their movement in my own body or see it in my mind's eye. I aim to deepen my supervisee's movement experience by offering my witnessing as a way of enabling them to become more consciously aware and deepen their own understanding of their movement experience. This embodied way of engaging with how my supervisee presents helps me to find an empathic and containing way of reflecting back to them what I see and feel in me. This supports the supervisee in accessing the symbolic material before it is articulated and before defence structures can be enacted. This type of inter-vention can create a feedback loop between supervisor and supervisee as they reflect together on the moment or movement chosen by the supervisee. Doing so helps to develop the reflective function within the supervisee.

For supervisees who use movement as their modality, a direct route to the wisdom of the body can be reached by moving with them as they hold an awareness of their supervisory question. Together supervisee and supervisor can swap between leading and following roles. Offering a slight shift in their speed or pace, how they shape their bodies or the flow of their movements,

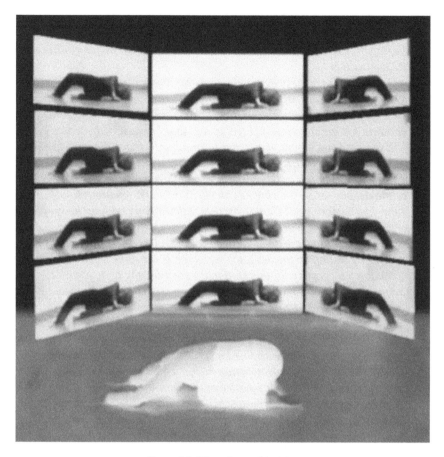

Figure 6.3 Mirroring and insight.

again before defensive structures have time to override the process, can enable new information or insight to become available to them.

Arrival of Insight

My fourth vignette addresses how insight can arise through mirroring and moving with the supervisee.

> *When I see Colette on the screen, I begin to attune to her and notice the differences within me and the space between us. I become aware of how still I feel within in relation to my busy and active supervisee and how this creates a sense of a gap between us. I have a sense that I want to expand this gap into a large space for us both to move in. I am pulled towards staying*

still and not speeding up to match her. Colette keeps playing with her screen so that I can 'better see her'. This draws me in closer to my screen and I lean forward, mirror neurons already firing. I sense her pace, her energy and the shaping of her body within me, all of it as if I am indeed shaping and moving like her, with her.

Colette moves and my eyes follow her. My body, although not moving, is activated and I can sense her movement patterns impacting on my physical body. I witness her as she moves and my body responds to this experience of following her actions closely. I feel in me what her own body actually does. A long slow lengthening of her right arm up into space, fingers extending, neck lengthening as her face turns towards and follows the stretch of the arm. I feel this in my own body as I sit quietly witnessing, not moving, just feeling the impact her moving has on me as my mirror neurons fire. At some point, I sit further back from the screen, allowing my body to be supported by the chair and allowing for space between us. Mirroring is taking place in me as I sit in stillness, witnessing. I notice what this offers me: seated in my chair, arms resting on my desk, the vertebrae in my spine feeling compacted by the force of gravity. In this stationary position, my body enjoys the sensation it receives as I watch Colette's slow stretch. I am immediately in contact with my need to lengthen out slowly, to untangle my muscles in a slow leisurely way, to let each vertebra separate, one by one. Simultaneously, I am reminded of my ability to reach and wonder what I might reach for right now in this session with this supervisee. What is she also reaching for? When we sit and she speaks to a movement, a moment she wants to explore, I listen. Then I share what I notice in me with the intention of helping to deepen her experience. I encourage her to explore her felt experience within. I give her time, allowing her to bring her conscious awareness into her reflection. She speaks to feeling more capable, of feeling she can now take her place in her team, no longer small and scared. We then move to relating insights to her practice.

As conscious awareness develops, a sense of clarity will often appear in the supervisee. The sense-making of the moment and the movement can offer something new, something unknown or more accurate as well as deeper understanding and insight.

Mirroring and Co-creation

In this fifth and final vignette, I explored an experience of mirroring when my supervisee, John, left his room to go and find items in response to his supervisory question.

I was sitting at my computer screen, still attuned to John after having invited him to go and collect objects to use for the creative exploration of his supervision dilemma. On this occasion I followed my own impulse to also go and find objects in relation to his supervision dilemma. I gathered my objects, holding John's check-in in mind and body. My supervisee arrives back with a long power cable all tangled up. We begin to explore what we notice and wonder about this together. I too had brought a bunch of tangled cables. The similarity in our objects strikes me, although I do not share mine at this moment. Once we finish exploring John's items, I present mine: the bunch of tangled cables and the bamboo bowl I had put them in. We explore the bowl, the container and the cables being contained. A moment of fresh insight arises in John: the need to contain more or create a clearer awareness of the container he already is, in order to hold the messier aspects of trans-ference and projection that he faces in his day-to-day work.

I am left curious about how such attunement is possible and the relationship to the concept of mirroring. *Is it possible that mirroring not only triggers a phys-ical action in the other but may also lead to a subconscious shared knowledge? Can we mirror beyond the physical?* The elusive aspects of the experiences that I present here really have me wondering: *what are the supervisor and supervisee co-creating?*

Conclusion

For supervisors who do not primarily follow a movement-based or body-oriented approach, becoming more consciously aware of the work of the mirror neurons may be a place to begin – an accessible place to start their exploration into embodied practice regardless of training and background.

The five vignettes offer the beginning of an exploration of the concept of mirroring in supervision. I also offer a video (Joseph, 2013, Appendix 1) where I share some of my experiences of mirroring. When viewing the video, I encourage the viewer to simply watch and notice their felt sense, their body's response, what catches their attention and wonder about. In doing so mirror neurons are activated. The video is a means of experiencing the impact of mirroring.

In this chapter, I have explored mirroring in supervision in the building of trusting relationships, in the offering of hospitality, the access to insight and support of group work. I have also touched on less clear areas such as when mirroring transcends the physical into the spaces before the session begins, pre-transference, as well as in exploring that which is being co-created between supervisor and supervisee. These are only some areas of supervision and of the supervisory relationship where mirroring may offer opportunities.

Although supervisors may already be using mirroring as a concept or intervention, this chapter offers a bridge between verbal and body-based practices. Researching mirroring in the context of supervision has enabled me to clarify my practice with supervisees who are familiar with psychotherapy and embodied forms of reflection, as well as with those unacquainted with supervision itself. In working with the concept of mirror neurons, I find I have the flexibility to deepen my offering as a supervisor even while working with those less experienced in embodied practices.

Appendix 1: An Exploration of An Embodied Sense of Mirroring

https://youtu.be/N_V8PfCf6oI
I recommend watching the video after having read this chapter.

The mirror sequence and group sequence are taken from an earlier piece of work (Joseph, 2013).

References

Adler, J. (2021). *A Brief Description of the Discipline of Authentic Movement*. Available at: https://disciplineofauthenticmovement.com

Arbib, M.A. (2002). Language evolution: the mirror system hypothesis, in M.A. Arbib (Ed.) *The Handbook of Brain Theory and Neural Networks* (2nd edn.). Cambridge, MA: MIT Press. 606–11.

Bergson, H. (1911). *The Selection of Images for Conscious Presentation: What Our Body Means and Does in Matter and Memory*. London: George Allen & Unwin. 1–85.

Bloom, K. (2006). *The Embodied Self: Movement and Psychoanalysis*. London: Karnac Books.

Cozoloni, L. (2014). *The Neuroscience of Human Relationships* (2nd edn.). London: Norton.

Farnsworth, J. (2010). Creative Supervision through Doubling, Mirroring and Role Reversal. Available at: https://aanzpa.org/wp-content/uploads/theses/121.pdf

Gallese, V. (2001). The 'shared manifold' hypothesis: From mirror neurons to empathy. In E. Thompson (Ed.) *Between Ourselves: Second-person Issues in the Study of Consciousness*. Exeter: Imprint Academic. 33–50.

Gendlin, E. (1981). *Focusing*. New York: Bantam Books.

Hawkins, P. & Shohet, R. (2012). *Supervision in the Helping Professions* (3rd edn.). Maidenhead: Open University Press.

Homann, K. (2017). Dynamic equilibrium: engaging neurophysiological intelligence through dance movement psychotherapy. In H. Payne (Ed.) *Essentials of Dance Movement Psychotherapy*. Oxon: Routledge. 37–51.

Jeannerod, M., Arbib, M.A., Rizzolatti, G. & Sakata, H. (1995). Grasping objects: the cortical mechanisms of visuomotor transformation. *Trends in Neurosciences*, 18(7): 314–20. DOI: 10.1016/0166-2236(95)93921-J

Joseph, J. (2013). A sense of holding. Available at: https://youtu.be/hvq3W1GBpq4

Joseph, J. & Karkou, V. (2017). Holding and adolescent angst. In H. Payne (Ed.) *Essentials of Dance Movement Psychotherapy*. Oxon: Routledge. 201–222.

Levy, F.J. (2005). *Dance Movement Therapy*. (2nd edn.) Virginia: National Dance Association American Alliance for Health, Physical Education, Recreation and Dance. 22–4.

Meekums, B. (1992). The love bugs. In H. Payne (Ed.) *Dance Movement Therapy: Theory and Practice* (1st edn.). London: Tavistock Routledge. 18–38.

Meekums, B. (2006). Embodiment in dance movement therapy training and practice. In H. Payne (Ed.) *Dance Movement Therapy: Theory, Research and Practice*. Hove: Routledge. 167–83.

Meekums, B. (2012). Kinaesthetic empathy and movement in dance movement psychotherapy. In D. Reynolds & M. Reynolds (Eds.) *Kinaesthetic Empathy in Creative and Cultural Practices*. Bristol, UK/Chicago, USA: Intellect. 51–65.

Moore, B. (2017). *Reflexive Supervision: A Workbook for Learning Within and Across Professions*. UK: CreateSpace, Amazon.

Paintner, C.V. & Beckman, B. (2010). *Awakening the Creative Spirit: Bringing the Arts to Spiritual Direction*. New York: Morehouse Publishing.

Pallaro, P. (1999). *Authentic Movement: Essays by Mary Starks Whitehouse, Janet Adler and Joan Chodorow*. London: Jessica Kingsley.

Paterson, M. (2020). *Between and Rock and a Hard Place: Pastoral Supervision Revisited and Revisioned*. UK: Amazon.

Payne, H. (2008). *Supervision of Dance Movement Psychotherapy: A Practitioner's Handbook*. East Sussex: Routledge.

Rizzolatti, G. & Arbib, M.A. (1998). Language within our grasp. *Trends in Neurosciences*, 21(5): 188–94. DOI: 10.1016/S0166-2236(98)01260-0

Rova, M. (2017). Embodying kinaesthetic empathy through interdisciplinary practice-based research. *The Arts in Psychotherapy*, 55: 164–73. DOI: 10.1016/j.aip.2017.04.008

Slochower, J.A. (1996). *Holding and Psychoanalysis: A Relational Perspective*. London: Routledge.

Winnicott, D.W. (1965). *The Maturational Processes and the Facilitating Environment*. London: Karnac Books.

Chapter 7

Reflections on Thresholds and Containers in Supervision

Céline Butté

Introduction

Over the years, I have grappled with a seemingly unreconcilable tension between spontaneity and structure, more specifically between dance and movement improvisation, and choreography. If improvisation was an image, it would be that of an old friend who welcomes me with open arms: no expectations, simply showing up, expressing what is alive in me and meeting what is evoked between me and 'the other'. It is an immensely freeing and restorative experience. Choreography, on the other hand, defines and organises bodies in space, offers focus, direction and engages consciousness from the word go. It is orienting and clarifying. During training and since qualifying as a psychotherapist and supervisor, the question of spontaneity and structure has remained an important source of inspiration. In this chapter, I reflect on this improvisation-structure continuum and present how movement improvisation, including everyday movement, dancing and organising the space, may enrich the embodied supervision process.

Facilitating a psychotherapeutic or supervisory process includes observing and listening so as to receive what is being expressed as well as guiding and directing. To do this, supervisors first create what I would refer to as a containing experience: a safe space where supervisees feel supported and able to be themselves, strengths and vulnerabilities included, without feeling judged. This is a psychological, emotional and pragmatic endeavour. It may be predictable and tangible (an agreed location and time) as well as elusive and unplanned.

Fundamentally, containers are framed by boundaries, which I prefer to call thresholds. (Etymologically speaking, 'boundary' invites a binding association, while 'threshold' is originated from the German 'tread', which invites movement in all sorts of directions). A concrete example of a threshold might be the moment my supervisee and I have entered the dance studio or consultation room and I have shut the door behind us, or the moment we see and hear one another during an online session. Both of us know what we have contracted for and are directing our attention to the task of supervision.

DOI: 10.4324/9781003034940-8

Together, we have stepped over a threshold that is both a physical reality, the room (real or virtual) we are in, and a psychological and cognitive experience, the directing of our focus towards the task at hand. A more elusive sense of a threshold may be when my supervisee and I sense and choose when the work has arrived somewhere helpful for this particular session. Whilst time – a concrete marker and container – always guides the holding of the arc of a session (Butté & Hoo, 2014: 132. Figure 7.1), closing the creative process and guiding the work towards a reflective dialogue is an art. This art, which I see as a dance of reciprocities between supervisor and supervisee(s), requires the crossing of several thresholds in such a way that the supervisee can safely delve into and emerge from the creative exploration enriched by the less cognitively driven time spent with their clinical material. Such explorations enable the supervisee to turn the volume down on their thinking for a while (during part three of the supervisory arc in particular) to then later re-engage their verbally reflective self more proactively so as to reap the fruit of the creative work undertaken within the thresholds provided. The latter taking place during parts four and five of the supervisory arc.

As a means of creative exploration, dance and movement improvisation give us access to a form of intelligence that bypasses cognitive processes, including words, to reach directly to the heart of the lived, felt experience (Reeve, 2021; Wengrower & Chaiklin, 2021). In this chapter, I illustrate how I use movement and dance improvisation within the threshold of supervision, to bring to the surface aspects of the work we did not know were needing attention (Best, 2008: 143) or that we did not know how to be with. I argue the role and value of stepping over the threshold between verbally articulating

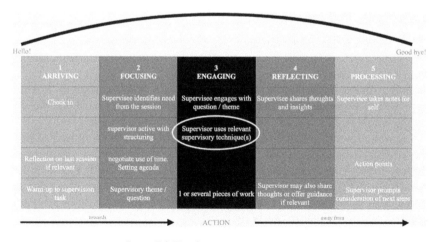

Figure 7.1 The five-part supervisory arc.

Source: Reproduced with Permission of Jessica Kingsley Publishers through PLSClear.

our reflection on practice issues and reflecting on these through dance and movement improvisation – and vice versa. Through vignettes from supervision of individuals and groups, I illustrate how dancing and movement improvisation may contain the reflective process and provide gateways to greater awareness and a source of nurture.

I work from the premise that the essence of supervision is to raise supervisees' awareness and develop their resilience (Hawkins & McMahon, 2020: xiv). Resilience is here understood as our capacity to identify challenges in our practice and attend to them in supervision (or other constructive reflective contexts) in order to return to the work with our clients with renewed energy and a greater sense of trust and clarity on how to hold them. In this chapter, I speak to embodied processes that enable us to get in touch with what is at play within and between us as supervisees and supervisors. Through creative and embodied frameworks, we re-present aspects of our experience with our clients and allow our attention to shift from a cognitively driven approach to reflection to a movement-based and sensory-oriented way of focusing our curiosity. Within and through our body, engaged spontaneously and creatively, we often find just what we need to return to our practice restored and inspired.

In the first section, I illustrate how our body never lies and how at times the embodied process brings the supervisee's focus where it needs to be, bypassing what their cognitive self might have thought priority. I then introduce FERN (a Framework for the Embodied Reflective Narrative), a supervision tool I developed over the years, which offers clear thresholds and containers for spontaneous movement and improvised dance in supervision.

The Body as a Compass

> We are threshold creatures
>
> (Hartley, 2020: 43)

Stepping into a dance studio is like looking at a blank canvas or a white page: full of promises, potentials, excitement and anxiety, I have not moved, yet my whole body is already there, orienting to its own reverie.

Spontaneous movement and dance improvisation enable an embodied process of free association that at times brings us to the bodymind[1] (Bainbridge Cohen, 1994; Aposhyan, 2004; Ablack, 2008; Westland, 2015; Payne, 2019) in such a way that the conscious mind does not enable. At times, this takes us to the most salient edges of our practice, where our attention and energy are needed. We cannot ignore our body.

Becca is part of an online supervision group attended by three dance movement (psycho)therapists[2]. The group checks in and soon agrees to take some time to turn to their own body, in their own space. I guide a process of landing in oneself, sensory awareness, and awareness of what feels needed. Inviting them to sense a particular tension, point of curiosity in their body and to notice from this place what they feel is calling for their attention. I facilitate a process of clarifying a supervisory question or theme.

Becca, when her turn comes, shares her question with the group. It is clear and relates to a specific client. I offer the group to follow the writing, moving and writing supervision framework developed by Heidrun Panhofer (Panhover, Payne & Meekums, 2011). Each takes about ten minutes to write in prosaic form whatever comes to mind in relation to their question: what they know about the client, the context, and what they feel could be helpful in their work with them. I then facilitate a ten-minute process of embodied inquiry and resonance with what they have just written. Following this, supervisees take a further ten minutes to write a poem that crystalises the essence of what the embodied inquiry has enabled them to contact. In the group's verbal reflections that follows, Becca is somewhat puzzled: although she had a clear question about a specific client, the process of having just ended her work with another client prior to this supervision session took over her embodied inquiry. She had no choice but to give way to this.

On this occasion, if there had not been the embodied process of inquiry, Becca might have taken more time to realise that she was dismissing this most recent ending with a client despite this having had a huge impact on her emotionally and physically. As Snowber tells us: 'It is living through and in the body that informs words' (2020: ix). How do we enable our supervisees to *live through* and be present in their body during supervision sessions? How do we facilitate a process through which they can remember what really needs attending to in relation to their practice? Sometimes, as in Becca's example, turning to free association through movement, dance and improvisation and offering bridges – another kind of threshold – that facilitate movement between conscious and unconscious material through tools such as Panhofer's writing, moving and writing process gives supervisees immediate access to pre-conscious knowing and countertransferential material (Panhover, Payne & Meekums, 2011). As this example illustrates, when we dare let the body lead the way, the body does present its wisdom to our consciousness.

Stepping over the threshold between cognitive attention (which includes verbal inquiry) and the non-verbal embodied realm of existence enables the supervisee to enter a process whereby the voice of the body can be listened to more acutely. I would argue that there are times in supervision when this is all that is required to direct our compass and attention where it is really needed. As supervisors, we need tools and methodologies to contain such a process. Panhofer's is one amongst many tools that facilitates such work.

In the next section of this chapter, I present another such framework where thresholds and containers for the embodied inquiry are this time concretised in space. The space is divided into sections, each offering a different locus to move into and through in order to creatively invest a supervisory dilemma from different perspectives.

FERN (Framework for the Embodied Reflective Narrative): A Creative Embodied Supervision Tool

It is through my input on the London Centre for Psychodrama (LCP) Creative Approaches to Supervision diploma that I first proposed this technique to contribute an embodied framework to the creative supervisor's toolbox. In the LCP supervision model, following an initial check-in and having arrived at a supervisory question or theme, the supervisor will often facilitate the supervision process by choosing from a variety of tools and techniques. This leads into the latter part of the session where the supervisee reflects on insights gained from the creative inquiry and how this will translate back in their practice. FERN is one of these tools. It is used at the heart of the supervision session, once supervisor and supervisee have identified a theme for further investigation and forms part three of the arc of a session (Figure 7.1). Through FERN the supervisor guides a focused embodied inquiry into the supervisory dilemma.

How FERN Evolved

Inspiration for FERN sprang from three concepts, the *participant-observer*, the role of *silent witness* from the Discipline of Authentic Movement (Adler, 2002) and *Embodied Performances* (Allegranti, 2011).

Inherent to the first placement experience of the Dance Movement Psychotherapy (DMP) trainee at Roehampton University, London, is the role of participant observer. During their first year of training, students are assigned a placement where the main aim is for them to attend sessions run by an experienced dance movement psychotherapist, observe and participate. Each student must work out exactly what this means to them in that particular context. During this placement, trainees are encouraged to be part of a DMP process without rushing into being useful or offering any activity or wise comment. I still remember my confusion at the paradox held in the term 'participant-observer' as I went through this experience in the early days of becoming a dance movement psychotherapist. Over time on this first placement, however, I began to realise that I was being invited to wonder and engage with what seemed to me to be a contradiction. This ingrained in me the notion that observing *is* participating and awakened my curiosity about what it means to be observing when actively participating (for example in a movement activity).

The use of the term observer/witness in FERN has certain similarities with the role of silent witness in the Discipline of Authentic Movement, a practice in which the relationship between a mover and a witness is fundamental. In FERN, it is the ability of the observer/witness to be embodied – to be conscious of how they feel as they see the other – that takes inspiration from the role of silent witness in the Discipline of Authentic Movement. In this movement practice, the silent witness has the opportunity to bring awareness to whatever is touched in them as they see the other – which may include judgements or projections – while being free of any responsibility to attend closely or speak to the mover. Similarly in FERN supervisees in the observer/ witness zone, seeing others but with no responsibility towards them, have the space to know their own experience more fully. In this outer circle, the supervisee is free to have their eyes closed or open, to be looking in or to be looking out. (Butté & Lavendel, teacher of the Discipline of Authentic Movement, personal conversation, 29 September 2021).

Embodied Performances is a feminist research and practice methodology developed by Beatrice Allegranti that integrates autobiographical, relational and political aspects of 'selves' in motion and 'allows a process of revisioning' (Allegranti, 2011: 499). In one of her presentations of *Embodied Performances*, Allegranti divides the space into three adjoining rectangles with yellow road hazard warning tape stuck to the ground (ibid: 52), which has the word 'caution' written on it. FERN is inspired by this division of the space into different zones and the notions of inquiring into autobiographical, relational and political aspects of selves. This is but my own interpretation of a fraction of Allegranti's work and not an attempt at adapting *Embodied Performances* as a whole, to supervision.

Allegranti was part of the teaching team on my journey to becoming a dance movement psychotherapist and, as far as I know, was pioneering performative forms of inquiry into the DMP world at the time (2001–02). She would often divide the space into specific zones, allocate them a title related to a particularly salient existential theme and invite trainees to invest these zones with spontaneous movement. This particular invitation to perform aspects of our identity and experience, on our own or simultaneously with peers, is another aspect of her work that inspires FERN.

How FERN Works

FERN invites the division of the space in four connected and distinct sections (Figure 7.2).

   Inner circle divided into three segments:
      Segment 1: Self
      Segment 2: Relationship
      Segment 3: Bigger Picture (sociopolitical and environmental)

   Outer circle: Observer/Witness

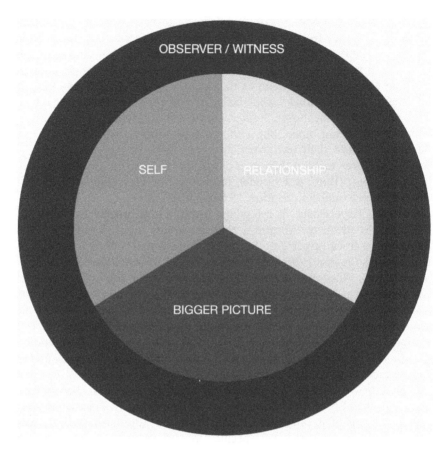

Figure 7.2 FERN as laid out in the space.

Setting FERN up in the space may be carried out by the supervisor alone whilst supervisees observe, in collaboration between supervisor and supervisees or by supervisees on their own (this works well online, for example as well as with supervisees already familiar with the structure).

Once the structure has been set up, the supervisor remains outside of it and guides the entire process from there. Supervisees are invited to physically visit each of the four sections (self, relationship, bigger picture and observer/witness) laid out on the floor. They may use spontaneous movement or dance, following their instincts and letting the body do the talking and the thinking. As supervisees invest in this framework, the supervisor may invite them to pay attention to their felt-sense, notice somatic and sensory experiences and attend to their posture and gestures. The supervisor may also ask if there is a desire to linger in a particular section, move quickly through it or pause, for example.

Supervisees take their time in and through each zone and let their question/ theme resonate. They are invited to let themselves be moved into each of the zones. Props (such as small objects or postcards) may be placed in the space to concretise (Chesner, 2019: 31) elements of their inquiry. Thus, supervisees give a physical form to aspects of their supervisory dilemma which they are now able to interact with. The space now invested lends itself to contemplation and play within which the story supervisees hold within themselves about their client or professional query becomes represented out there. Free association through such symbolic play frees up new ways of seeing and being with what may at first have felt challenging or unclear.

Using FERN in an Ongoing Group[3]

Nine participants attend this supervision group; all of them are trained dance movement therapists. We have been working together in a large studio space for several months; this is the third of our planned schedule of intensive supervision weekends. During one of our sessions, after everyone has clarified their supervisory question or theme, I propose that we use FERN as a way of working simultaneously. Together we take the time to co-create this framework using scarves and other objects available to delineate each of the four zones. Once we are all satisfied, I invite the group to wander in the structure, reminding them of what each zone represents. I then suggest that they use movement and props to invest the structure with their supervision question. The framework comes to life. One supervisee lies down in the self zone, closes their eyes and stays there for a while: another hovers over the boundary between the self and relationship zones. Several supervisees meet in the bigger picture zone where some interact with one another right away whilst others remain immersed in their own exploration. I also notice a few supervisees standing and sitting in the observer/witness zone. Some have closed their eyes whilst others are taking in what is happening in the central three segments. Later the boundaries come to life as the non-verbal creative exploration unfolds. Supervisees take ownership of the framework and place props in each zone. When one participant leaves a prop in a particular location, another places another object in relation to this prop. Then a moment later a supervisee plays on one of the scarves that makes the boundary between the self and the relationship zones. I can see how much they are getting immersed into the sensations that the texture the scarf offers and how freeing it is to be letting their body move from these inner somatic resonances. This seems to give permission to others to engage both with other boundaries made of scarves as well as with some of the props located within each zone. They are at times playful and mischievous and at others deeply attentive. Vocal expression also become part of the creative process, offering a spontaneous means of communication between some participants. One moment the space fills up with bold and loud sounds and minutes later all that can be heard is everyone's breathing. I let the group proceed with their embodied inquiry for about twenty minutes. Engaged with ease, I can see that they are immersed in the moment.

Reflections on the process, as we close this session, highlight the value of investing this structure as a group and of engaging with the three inner sections (self, relationship and bigger picture) as well as taking time in the observer/witness outer section, either looking in on the inner circle and letting resonances unfold, or tuning in to self to regulate when necessary.

This is a session that takes place in a country where dance movement therapy is an emergent profession and where the question of professional boundaries and professional identity is raw and alive in each participant. The structure enabled a collective meeting point with this theme and frank discussions about the challenges all were facing ensued, as a group of dance movement therapists as well as in relation to their individual circumstances. For my part, this is the first time I witnessed such embodied enthusiasm and spontaneity with this framework. The insights that follow are a testimony to the deep restorative and complementary nature of both framing and directing the inquiry, as well as letting the group spontaneously engage with the structure as a whole, including its boundaries.

As the example above illustrates, in dividing the space, FERN creates thresholds and containers to focus and locate specific aspects of a supervision inquiry. The somatic- and movement-based creative exploration invites supervisees to step into the 'as if' in a structured and focused way. For example, the self zone gives permission to express and clarify what is being evoked physically, emotionally and psychologically on an autobiographical level. Marked by ribbons or scarves laid on the ground, the threshold into another zone is visible and invites a conscious act of transitioning from one particular way of resonating with a supervisory theme or question into another. Stepping into another zone can be quite evocative as is illustrated above by the supervisee spending time at a particular threshold. During the embodied inquiry, supervisees are encouraged to be mindful of and interact with these thresholds. The supervisor may ask: 'What are they made of?', 'Are they rigid, porous, an open window or a locked door?', 'What does it feel like to stay at a particular threshold?', 'Should you cross over?' At the point of arriving and being in a new zone, new sensations, feelings, thoughts and images arise, directly evoked by the embodied experience of having moved from one section of the frame into another. The same clarifying and permissive principle goes on as supervisees are encouraged to progress through the whole framework.

Each Section in More Detail

Self: Within this zone the supervisee is 'with' and gives shape to the self of the therapist/supervisee or the self of their client or other 'selves' relevant to the supervisory question.

Relationship: This area invites attention to any possible relational dynamic relevant to the supervisory question. Specific people may be located, represented or embodied. Or, particular aspects of significant relational dynamics may be given shape.

Bigger picture: This area encompasses both the socio-political context and environmental factors. It may refer to a particular system, family, culture or organisation relevant to the supervisory question as well as a physical location of a piece of work or other significant environmental factors. Here, supervisees may embody or represent the system(s) within which the inquiry is embedded as well as the actual place(s) where the work takes place.

Observer/witness: Here the supervisee is invited to pay attention to what is going on in themselves as well as within the rest of the structure, with gentle curiosity. They can also regulate in this zone, either on their own or with the help of the supervisor. Taking a mindful and conscious step back from the immersive experience of the other three zones helps gain some distance from the immediacy and intensity of that which has emerged. Supervisees may close their eyes, catch their breath, look at, feel and sense what is there, both literally and symbolically. Sometimes we get overwhelmed with an experience, in particular if working with an embodied form of inquiry that is not familiar, and we need to orient away from it.

It must be stated that the observer/witness zone is not a place of numbing or collapse. It is a safe non-judgemental space of noticing, with kindness and compassion, what is going on in oneself, and if used with a group, what is going on in the three segments of the inner circle.

For supervisees, stepping into this structure is often surprisingly powerful; knowing that the way in and out of the central three sections is via this regulatory, observer/witness zone provides safety in the process. Whilst the inner frames of the self, relationship and bigger picture invite spontaneous action, the outer frame of observer/witness encourages a deepening of awareness. In settling down in this zone, supervisees are invited to let the ripples from the more activating investigative zones of self, relationship and bigger picture land whilst retaining some form of engagement.

The observer/witness zone may also be seen as a form of buffer, as it is helpful to transition in and out of an embodied form of inquiry incrementally. This outer zone surrounding the inner three segments is a reminder neither to abandon the inner inquiry nor to abruptly transition away from the immediacy of the activation that the inner circle potentially invites.

With practice, supervisees become able to see themselves with more clarity (enabled, often, by less self-judgement), thus allowing them to know more clearly their experience with their clients. Engaging with the observer/witness zone invites supervisees to cultivate an inner supervisor (Payne, 2001; Casement, 1985, 1990).

Ways in which FERN May Be Used

FERN can be used with individuals and groups, in person as well as online.

It is a matrix through and within which new possibilities may be felt, sensed, expressed, embodied, narrated and witnessed. Whilst I recommend that the bare bone of the structure is used exactly as presented (Figure 7.2), this structure is quite versatile and offers infinite ways to inquire within it. As they step into each of the different zones, supervisees may walk and talk through the process; alternatively, verbal communication may be kept to a minimum. Through this framework, supervisees give way to a spontaneous performance of identity – private and public (Allegranti, 2011). Through visiting each of the four distinct sections, they can tell a story about a supervisory dilemma, by giving physical form to and moving with and through different perspectives on their dilemma. By having invested each of the different zones, they expand or narrow their focus down and can play with different ways of inquiring into what they feel challenged by in their practice. Visiting each section enables an embodied immersion into the supervisory theme or question from a specific perspective and provides the supervisee with immediate access to countertransferential material (Panhofer, Payne & Meekums, 2011).

Supervisees who are not particularly comfortable with movement improvisation may be invited to sit on a chair that they place in each zone and take a posture from each different perspective. Postcards, scarves or small objects that particularly resonate with the theme being explored may also be used.

When working in person and with a group, everyone may focus on one question and work simultaneously. Alternatively, each supervisee may invest the structure with their own supervisory question whilst all work alongside one another.

Following the embodied process, supervisees are invited to reflect. They may discuss in pairs or write answers focusing on all or some of the following questions: 'Did you noticing a particular zone of preference or aversion?', 'What did you notice about your own exploration of the witness/observer zone?', 'How does the sequence in visiting different zones inform your reflection?'

Emerging from FERN

Objects and props – as well as the space – are significant parts of the process of using creative techniques in psychotherapy and in supervision. In the context of FERN, objects and props also have great importance, as each invests the space with a frame that represents a particular aspect of an inquiry. Therefore, to mark the conclusion of the session, the supervisory space should be cleared of all objects and any props that had been used to mark sections be returned to where they were picked up from. In this way, the objects, props and the space are de-roled (Chesner, 2019: 42), a term which acknowledges that as soon as an object has been used to create a frame or concretise a particular aspect of an inquiry, it is imbued with a specific role, or en-roled. Once the objects, props and the space have been de-roled, the group is ready to gather for concluding reflections, first, in relation to their supervisory question and, second, on the process of using FERN.

Both en-roling and de-roling are thresholds towards and away from action, as represented by the central third part of the supervisory arc (Figure 7.1). During those transitions, supervisor and supervisees attend to the ritual of gathering objects, orienting towards (en-roling) and away from (de-roling) the use of a creative technique. The concrete aspect of this ritual represented by the use of objects and the movement of supervisees in space creates a sacred and precious moment in time. In the example of using FERN, supervisees are warming up and taking ownership of the framework when laying the structure on the ground as they walk around, choose scarves, cloths or ribbons, put them down and adjust them. After the immersive experience of using FERN to focus on their supervisory question, the clearing of the space is another opening of a space in time during which supervisees quietly let the creative exploration settle within themselves. This moment is a breathing space during which the embodied reflective process is active in the back-ground. Feelings, sensations, thoughts and images bubble up without any conscious effort for this to happen and new meaning may arise. The ritual of clearing the space enables supervisees to do what they need to do to emerge from the immersive experience of investing the creative framework and orient towards a more reflective place in themselves, 'honouring the power of the unconscious imagery' and 'of the healing power of symbols and metaphors' (Chesner & Zografou, 2014: 38). If such de-roling hygiene is not attended to, supervisees run the risk of remaining caught in or overly identified with a particular aspect of their inquiry, which affects their reflective capacity. On the contrary, when de-roling has taken place, supervisees experience a returning to the dialogical place they were in at the start of the session at a physical, emotional and cognitive level. This return, informed by the ripples of the creative investigation, is all the richer when the de-roling ritual has been completed fully.

Using FERN Online

In my initial contract with supervisees who seek individual or group supervision online, I offer a detailed list of objects to gather for our work together. This list includes scarves, ribbons, cloths, cards, postcards and small objects. So when they arrive at a session, supervisees have, in their own way, warmed up to being supervised through a creative method and have some objects available to them including those relevant to laying out FERN.

Figure 7.3 shows a supervisee, who has her own studio, in an individual supervision session online. Of course, supervisees do not always have the use of an entire studio, and whilst the laying out of FERN requires space, it has been used successfully in rooms with smaller dimensions, such as an office. When working in a smaller space, the use of postures and gestures may be more suitable. This does not take away the potency of the framework as postures can be deeply evocative.

As a supervisor working online, I am not physically in the room and thus not fully available to facilitate co-regulation if needed. In this case, the observer/witness zone becomes even more important as it offers a buffer and opportunity to regulate as described above. Through this observer/witness zone, supervisees are able to look after themselves whilst I am on the other side of the screen, at times guiding them to this zone if I have sensed a need for them to step away from the immersive experience in a particular inner segment.

Working with groups online, FERN may be used in a very similar way to meeting a group in a studio. Online or in person, we may have chosen to focus on one participant's question only or each may be working simultaneously in their own space, particularly if there is a shared group theme.

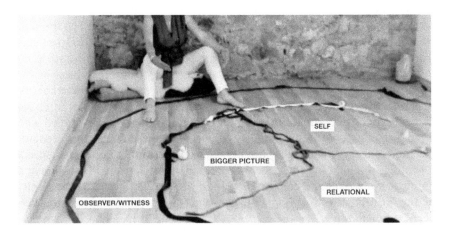

Figure 7.3 FERN during an online 1:1 session. Photograph by the author.

When focusing on one individual within a group, I will talk through the structure first, especially if it is not familiar. Then I will invite all but the supervisee whose question has been chosen, to switch their video and audio off but to remain present and attentive to their peer. Once the peer whose supervisory dilemma has been focused on has completed the whole FERN process, I give them time to de-role the space and invite the rest of the group to turn their video and audio back on. I offer the supervisee who has just finished their piece of work the opportunity to hear from their peers. Sometimes this is important but sometimes they prefer to consider their piece of work complete once they have de-roled. Both options are welcome and part of the transition away from the immersive experience of using this creative technique.

The final part of the work is an invitation to all those who have observed their peer's piece of work, to turn their focus back to their own question or theme and reflect on it in the light of the work they have observed. It is often the case that something has been useful in the work witnessed, even if on the face of things their question and that of their peer felt very different.

Concluding Remarks on the Use of FERN as a Supervision Tool

FERN offers aesthetic hygiene or 'structural hygiene' (Chesner and Zografou, 2014: 38) for an embodied creative supervision process. The defined physical space becomes a matrix or container for a supervision dilemma. Each zone comes to life as supervisees position, locate, step towards and away, around, and in and out of the different segments and whatever object is placed in this framework for them to engage with. In the moment of the embodied inquiry, the felt sense and resonance with the delineated distinct zones come to the fore. The intention is to invite a deconstruction of a supervision dilemma and a re-membering and re-visioning. All becomes important and organised as awareness is brought to life from different perspectives. This yields clarity and discernment in response to a supervisory dilemma. Our body is knowledge. FERN is a framework through which we access this knowledge in service of a supervision issue. It favours a bottom-up approach (Ogden, Minton & Pain, 2006; Van Der Kolk, 2015; Levine, 2010; Rothschild, 2000) whereby expression through movement, acknowledgement of sensations and images are for a moment at least, prioritised over a familiar narrative held within our cognition about a situation.

An Emerging Methodology

During a recorded interview with Beatrice Allegranti as part of my research towards this chapter (Butté & Allegranti, personal interview, 24 April 2020), I reflected on how her work influenced me to develop FERN. This conversation challenged me to clarify my intention around whether I was presenting a tool or a methodology. The further I engaged with this chapter, the more

I realised that I was in fact looking to articulate something greater, that is, to share my reflections on the versatility, changeability and sacred nature of the thresholds we may offer and invite our supervisees to cross. As such clear guided processes may enable them to safely make space for their own embodied experience in service of understanding their practice better.

As the above section illustrate, FERN is indeed a tool for clinical supervision. However, this writing process has elucidated that it may also be used as a methodology. The three inner segments and the outer circle that make up FERN (Figure 7.2) may be held in mind by the supervisor and used as a way to either facilitate a somatic- or movement-based inquiry or reflect on an improvised movement piece of work related to one's practice. Whilst it may be laid out in the space as a concrete framework, it may also be held in mind as a methodology when facilitating a supervisory process.

FERN used as a tool or as a methodology facilitates an enlivened connection through somatic attention and movement activation, illuminating a previously disregarded facet of our practice into our consciousness (Alvesson & Skoldberg (2000) in Dymoke, 2021).

A Note on Working With Improvised Movement

The level of guidance the supervisor must offer depends on the confidence supervisees have in working through improvised movement. If needed, at times I may invite supervisees to play by repeating, amplifying and making their movement, gestures or postures smaller (Allegranti, 2011). At other times I may invite them to be curious about their embodied process and what qualities of movement they are engaging with. Are they *yielding, pushing, reaching, grabbing* or *pulling,* or a combination of these? These developmental movement patterns offer a simple language to articulate and track the physical experience (Bainbridge Cohen, 1994; Loutsis, 2017). Alternatively, I may invite supervisees to pay attention to body sensations, movement, images, emotions and thoughts: a particular way of inquiring into the embodied process inspired by the *Building Blocks of Present Moment Experience* from Sensorimotor Psychotherapy (Ogden, Minton & Pain, 2006: 199).

Conclusion

> Our reflections are stories of resistance and possibilities
>
> (Johns, 2009: 4)[4]

Containers are made of boundaries or thresholds. In order to create safe containers for the dancing-improvising body in supervision, one must hold a clear thread of the territory that is being invested. Thresholds are also sacred (Reeve, 2014). 'What gets opened gets closed' is a simple principle that acts as a grounding guide in my practice, as illustrated by the different shades of the supervisory arc (Figure 7.1). If, for example, I see supervisees immersing themselves into movement as they arrive in the studio, I may encourage this, as well as a transition to checking in and naming what might have come up in the movement that is relevant to their clinical practice. I am constantly navigating the threshold in and out of the embodied creative process towards a conscious naming of themes or insights or alternatively from naming of a question towards an embodied improvised form of inquiry. Sometimes the territory for the embodied process of inquiry is strongly defined by the supervisees, in particular with supervisees who come from a preference towards kinaesthetic engagement (true of many dance movement (psycho) therapists). Other times I will proactively invite supervisees to delineate this territory, for example through the use of FERN as a tool. Whatever the way in and out of the embodied creative process, there *is* a way in and a way out, and thresholds to negotiate. This systematic attention to aesthetics is physically, psychically and spiritually essential as it directly nurtures the safety and value of supervision.

Symbolic or concrete, thresholds become containers of the immersive and evocative qualities of an embodied creative process from which the supervisee arises with renewed energy and insights that they can feel, sense and verbally articulate.

Van der Kolk's famous words 'the body keeps the score' (2015) are as true for psychotherapy as they are for supervision. Dance and movement are my frames of reference and I have argued here how they may be integrated as valuable elements in supervision. In the paragraphs above, I introduced how and when the unique performative, non-verbal and poetic qualities of this art form may enrich the supervisory process. I anticipate that the work presented will be of interest to dance movement psychotherapists as well as supervisors interested in incorporating embodied approaches in their practice.

Notes

1   The concept of bodymind has been written about at length for the past few decades and more profusely over the past ten years or so. The term challenges the idea of body mind dualism and argues that in essence (and put very simplistically) the body is held in mind, consciously or unconsciously and that our physical being can be considered as having a mind of its own. The spelling varies from body mind to bodymind, at times capitalised, at times not and has given way to numerous approaches to somatic and psychotherapy interventions such as Body Mind Centering (Bainbridge Cohen, 1994) Body-Mind Psychotherapy (Aposhyan, 2004), the BodyMind Approach (Payne, 2019) to name but a few and is also written about more conceptually (Ablack, 2008). Bodymind as a term is getting more and more integrated in wider scholarly and activist circles such as queer and disability studies (Clare, 2017).

2   In the UK the recognised terminology is *dance movement psychotherapy*, in the rest of the world; however, various terminologies are used and the use of the term *psychotherapy* is prohibited. As I work online with practitioners both based in the UK and abroad, the option *dance movement (psycho)therapy* feels honouring of these variations of recognised and accepted professional titles.
3   This is a composite vignette inspired from practice across Europe.
4   Copyright 2022 Wiley. Used with permission from Johns, C. *Becoming a Reflective Practitioner* (3rd edn). Wiley-Blackwell.

References

Ablack, C. J. (2008). The body-mind dynamics of working with diversity. In L. Hartley (Ed.) *Contemporary Body Psychotherapy. The Chiron Approach*. London: Routledge. 121–32.

Adler, J. (2002). *Offering from the Conscious Body: The Discipline of Authentic Movement*. Rochester, Vermont: Inner Traditions.

Allegranti, B. (2011). *Embodied Performances. Sexuality, Gender, Bodies* . London: Palgrave Macmillan.

Alvesson, M. & Skolberg. K. (2000). *Reflexive Methodology. New Vistas for Qualitative Research*. London: Sage Publications.

Aposhyan, S. (2004). *Body-Mind Psychotherapy. Principles, Techniques, and Practical Applications*. London: W. W. Norton.

Bainbridge Cohen, B. (1994). *Sensing, Feeling and Action. The Experiential Anatomy of Body Mind Centering*. Northampton, MA: Contact Editions.

Best, P. (2010). Observing interactions being shaped: Multiple perspectives within supervision. In S. Bender (Ed.) *Movement Analysis and Interaction*. Berlin: Logos Verlag. 257–68.

Best, P. (2008). Interactive reflections: moving between modes of expression as a model for supervision. In H. Payne (Ed.) *Supervision of Dance Movement Psychotherapy. A Practitioner's Handbook*. New York: Routledge. 137–53.

Butté, C & Hoo, F. (2014). Embodiment and Movement in Supervision: An Integration of Theories and Techniques from Body-oriented, Movement-based Psychotherapy and Supervision. In A. Chesner & L. Zografou (Eds.) *Creative Supervision across Modalities. Theory and Applications for Therapists, Counsellors and Other Helping Professionals*. London: Jessica Kingsley. 127–44.

Casement, P. (1985). *On Learning from the Patient*. London: Routledge.

Casement, P. (1990). *Further Learning from the Patient: The Analytic Space and Process*. London: Routledge.

Clare, E. (2017). *Brilliant Imperfection. Grappling with Cure*. USA: Duke University Press.

Chesner, A. (Ed.) (2019). *One-to-One Psychodrama Psychotherapy. Applications and Techniques*. London: Routledge.

Chesner, A. & Zografou, L. (Eds.) (2014). *Creative Supervision across Modalities. Theory and Applications for Therapists, Counsellors and Other Helping Professionals*. London: Jessica Kingsley.

Dymoke, K. (2021). *The Impact of Touch in Dance Movement Psychotherapy. A Body-Mind Centering Approach*. London: Intellect Books.

Hartley, L. (2020). Woman, body, earth and spirit: Journeys of descent through myth, embodiment and movement practice. In A. Williamson & B. Sellers-Young (Eds.) *Spiritual Herstories. Call on the Soul in Dance Research.* Bristol: Intellect. 35–68.

Hawkins, P. & McMahon, A. (2020). *Supervision in the Helping Professions* Maidenhead: Open University Press.

Johns, C. (2009). *Becoming a Reflective Practitioner* (3rd edn.). Chichester: Wiley-Blackwell.

Levine, P. (2010). *In an Unspoken Voice. How the Body Releases Trauma and Restores Goodness.* Berkeley, CA: North Atlantic Books.

Loutsis, A. (2017). Body, movement and trauma. In R. Hougham & B. Jones (Eds.) *Dramatherapy. Reflections and Praxis.* London: Palgrave. 145–68.

Ogden, P. Minton, K. & Pain, C. (2006). *Trauma and the Body. A Sensorimotor Approach to Psychotherapy.* USA: Norton.

Panhofer, H., Payne, H & Meekums, B. (2011). Dancing, moving and writing in clinical supervision? Employing embodied practices in psychotherapy supervision. *The Arts in Psychotherapy.* 38(1): 9–16. DOI: 10.1016/j.aip.2010.10.001

Payne, H. (2001). Authentic movement and supervision. e-motion, *ADMT-UK Newsletter*, Winter, 13(4): 4–7.

Payne, H. (2019). The bodymind approach and people affected by medically unexplained symptoms / somatic symptom disorder. In H. Payne, S. Koch, J. Tantia & T. Fuch (Eds.) *The Routledge International Handbook of Embodied Perspectives in Psychotherapy. Approaches from Dance Movement and Body Psychotherapies.* Oxon and New York: Routledge. 195–203.

Reeve, S. (Ed.) (2021). *Body and Awareness.* Axminster, UK: Triarchy Press.

Reeve, S. (2014). The sacrum and the sacred: mutual transformation of performer and site through ecological movement in a sacred site. In G. Williamson, G. Bateson, S. Whatley, S. & R. Weber (Eds.) *Dance, Somatics and Spirituality. Contemporary Sacred Narratives.* Bristol, UK: Intellect. 419–36.

Rothschild, B. (2000). *The Body Remembers. The Psychophysiology of Trauma and Trauma Treatment.* New York, USA: Norton.

Snowber, C. (2020). Dancing incantations. Preface to *Spiritual Herstories. Call on the Soul in Dance Research.* Bristol: Intellect. ix–xiii.

Van Der Kolk, B. (2015). *The Body Keeps the Score. Brain, Mind and Body in the Healing of Trauma.* New York, USA: Penguin Books.

Wengrower, H. & Chaiklin, S. (2021). *Dance and Creativity with Dance Movement Therapy. International Perspectives.* New York: Routledge.

Westland, G. (2015). *Verbal and Non-Verbal Communication in Psychotherapy.* London: W. W. Norton.

Chapter 8

Supervision Beyond Supervision
Widening and Nourishing Embodied Reflexivity as Part of Self-supervision

Roz Carroll

> *The phenomenal body is the central reference point acting as a somatic knowledge bank.*
>
> (Best, 2008: 150)

Being a therapist is a vocation, involving participation in others' lives in a way which requires both great openness and quiet reserve and reflection. It asks for deep human participation and a capacity for subtle responses arising from our sensitivity to the moment-by-moment context. Today it increasingly feels like a political activity; although I work with individual clients, I feel a connection to the sociopolitical context (lykou, 2021) and the collective – of history, and now – and that is also part of what I need to digest[1].

Most supervision is actually self-supervision. We start out being supervised fairly intensively and then as we become more experienced we have the freedom to create our own supervision structures. This may involve formal supervision, peer work, occasional consultation or other modes of supervision. It is these other modes – 'supervision beyond supervision' – that I want to reflect on in this chapter. In addition to one-to-one supervision with a Dance Movement Psychotherapist and regular peer supervision, I recognise a variety of supports for my personal self-supervision. These include cooking, walking in the park, reading or listening to (audio) novels, dance classes and being in ongoing Authentic Movement groups. All of these create facilitative spaces for me to reflexively process my clinical work in ways that are both generative and restorative.

Self-supervision incorporates self-regulation. *'Do I need to ground myself, digest my experience of the countertransference, wrestle with a particular dilemma?' or 'access my creativity, get into flow, capture images and details hovering on the edge of my consciousness?' 'Do I need a breathing space or a grieving space? Do I need to research or draw on theory?'*

Sometimes after my last client goes I descend to the kitchen and pick up an onion and start chopping and sautéing, not even knowing what I am going to cook. I love the earthy smell, the rhythmic action and the familiarity of a ritual of transformation from removing papery skin, to handling crisp,

DOI: 10.4324/9781003034940-9

pungent layers which quickly become softening aromatic bodies juxtaposed in the pan. I land quickly, and somewhere between not-thinking but just doing, and being consumed with whatever is in my body from the day's sessions. I relax. I free-associate through the fridge, gathering bits and pieces, slicing, tossing, sprinkling, adding dollops of this or that. Breathing steadies. I trust this process, and it enables me to start focusing on details from sessions, perhaps making notes, or just leaving perceptions to cook quietly, knowing they will evolve and settle.

Embodied Reflexivity

Elaboration is a key tool of supervision – the back and forth between supervisor and supervisee(s) is a creative dialogue of questioning, reflecting, tracking felt changes and gestures, moving and commenting in joint free-association. In self-supervision, this may occur internally in a more fragmented or fluid way. The rhythms of this reflexive process may vary – emerging intermittently, in forceful gushes of impact and recognition, or in dribbles of slowly connecting association.

> *On the morning of a session where I was due to meet a client whom I felt I had let down badly, I awoke with the word 'debacle' on my lips, as if from a dream. I grimaced at the appropriateness of the word but then, curious about its origins, I looked it up:*

Debacle

1   A sudden, disastrous collapse, downfall, or defeat; a disorderly retreat;
2   *A total, often ludicrous, failure;*
3   *The breaking up of a natural dam, usually made of ice, by a river and the ensuing rush of water* debacles, *The Free Dictionary* (n.d.)

> *I realised my unconscious had given me a gift. My client had made it clear she saw me as inept (ludicrous failure). Several times with this client I had experienced a collapse, an overwhelming sense of being defeated to the point of incapacity. But the image of the breaking up of ice in a river offered me a vivid metaphor. The client had been 'unfreezing' from long term trauma and consequently had a heightened sensitivity to misattunement. Having failed her more than once already, I was flooded with traumatic shame which left me floundering in a crucial moment. My clumsy response created a catastrophic sense, for her, of history repeating.*

Embodied reflexivity is a *loop*: a complex sequence of sensations, feelings and images that are digested and reflected upon, with formulations and understandings that are revised and recalibrated, over and over. As Shoshi

Asheri says, 'It's a bottom up process – the reflexivity or the mentalisation is guided and monitored by an embodied experience (…) moment to moment' (Asheri & Carroll, 2015). Ideally the fluidity of embodied thinking is held within an ethical intention of rigorous self-scrutiny[2]. 'Critical analysis requires the ability to shift one's position in such a way that one can see how one is being pressured, pushed, shaped by either dominant discourses, or particular contexts or roles' (Best, 2008: 140). This reflexive loop may be nourished by any phenomena if we are open to it: surprising synchronicities – like a song heard on the radio or a newspaper article – that seem charged with particular meaning.

Whilst the work of therapy is full of rich reward in terms of human contact, and engagement in intricate webs of relating and imagining, it can also place immense demands on our own capacity to process emotion. I am writing now in the time of Covid-19, Black Lives Matter, Climate Change and Refugees-in-crisis: multiple global humanitarian and ecological emergencies. The trans-mission of traumatic states from one body to another requires us to have a range of resources for self-regulating. The therapist has to allow herself to be impacted, and let this feed into and sustain a creative relational exploration. Immersion in groups, or with individual clients in many sessions a week, combined with our own busy and full lives, leads to the risk of burnout. One of my inspirations here is the feminist activist definition of 'radical self-care' as self-preservation in the context of political struggle (Lorde, 1988: 130).

Recuperation in the Park

Sometimes in a gap between clients, I will slip off to the park to 'commune' (Old French 'to share') with the wisest peers of all … the birds, the trees, the clouds in the sky, the earth under my feet. In summer I may walk barefoot. I look up at the birds and allow my eye to rest on their flight path, extending my vision further out. Whatever intensity I have been sharing in the room with my clients has more space around it and less pressure. I can walk briskly or wander in a meditative state, losing myself in the fragrance of flowers or affirming my substance as my heel hits the path. As Best comments 'We are changing perceptual positions by changing our position in the physical or in the social-relational space' (Best, P. personal communication, 23 March 2022).

This is even more crucial when working long hours in front of a screen while using online platforms which demand 'directed attention' even whilst we try to maintain the wider, softer, more open attention that embodied psy-chotherapy requires (Carroll, 2021: 4). Walking in a park or a wood allows us to switch focus and yield to a rich sensory space where attention can move without constraint (Duncan, 2018). For me, watching birds, freeing my eyes to shift upward, can be an immediate doorway into a more fluid state.

'Ecological movement' as described by Sandra Reeve, 'begins with the indi-vidual (…) becoming aware of the structure of the living body in movement'

(2008: 75). I expand my field of observation as I move in relation to trees, plants and the wider landscape. What I carry from my clinical work shifts and re-organises as I find new rhythms and shapes. I traverse, I am embraced, I follow light through the leaves. The semi-conscious orientation to this path which goes down to the pond, or this group of beech and ash trees, or this colourful rhododendron circle, is a dialogue of inner and outer. There are crossovers in perception which enhance the sense of dynamic interconnection between inner and outer worlds, such as catching sight of a squirrel darting up a tree at a particular moment when my own thoughts are quickening suddenly.

As the Coronavirus crisis began to escalate in March 2020, I was doing clinical work, supervision and teaching online. I began to experience – along with and through clients, colleagues, students and friends – the waves of dread, sadness and confusion that were spreading through the country. I found myself at times stunned, overwhelmed, exhausted: saturated with holding the intensity and scale of it.

My walks in the local park became more important.

> *My feet find the solid earth of the path. I feel shipwrecked, as if I am staggering on to the beach after nearly drowning. My chest feels full of grief, and a sense of 'this is too much'. Not for me personally but for those bearing the brunt of the virus tsunami: the unprotected, like the newly-qualified nurse on the Covid ward I had just heard about. My heart is beating fast and my limbs are heavy. With an effort I look up at the trees that line the path – the sycamore, oak and horse chestnut. Their quiet height helps me find my bearings.*
>
> *I walk along the path for a while, stumbling slightly. I duck into a place behind the trees, along a wall at the edge of the park. I am flanked by brick and wood. My hand finds the roughness of a tree trunk and I pause, finding support. It becomes easier to breathe. I let sensations of fear flood through me. I reach my arms around the tree and hold tight briefly, gratefully. I look up through the branches and the underside of the leaves seeing the patterning of light. My perspective is shifting, the intensity easing; rays of insight penetrating. I recognise now that this overwhelm derives not just from what I have taken in, but also from anticipating what might happen next. I, like so many, have got caught in over-identifying with the media driven narrative of rolling Covid-related disaster.*
>
> *I deliberately sense into my feet, feel the weight of gravity. Then I notice the variable trills of blue tits nearby, and my heart lifts.*

Through interactions that are kinaesthetic, tactile and affective, a new space opens up. The natural world is a co-therapist (Jordan, 2014) and a co-supervisor.

The lens of psychotherapy includes the client in culture and society, and now – in the growing field of eco-psychotherapy – the living environment. Self-supervision is leading me to initiate a new journey: to move toward outdoor work (Reeve, 2011) and re-view the practice of psychotherapy as situated in a wider ecology (Carroll, 2020).

Fiction as a Resource, as Research

Both the ethical imperative for an ever-broader range of social and cultural awareness and my personal desire for such demand a heightened effort of self-education (Butté & Evertsen 2020: 136). Reading can give us access to decolonised, queered and uniquely insightful narratives of multiple others in all kinds of context, such as Bernadine Evaristo's *Girl, Woman, Other* (2019). It can expand our frame of understanding by directly penetrating our embodied inner world: 'the 'voice' of the novelist heard through the voices of characters produces an uncanny sense of felt presence when it enters, disturbingly or consolingly, into the internal conversation that all of us have with ourselves, as we reframe and filter our experience' (Waugh, 2015: 49). This felt presence can be so strong that finishing a novel can leave me aching for the characters and the world I have shared with them, grieving the loss of that ongoing participation.

As the psychoanalyst Deleuze astutely observed, 'Artists are clinicians, not with respect to their own case, nor even with respect to a case in general; rather, they are *clinicians of civilisation*' (Deleuze 1969: 237 in Waugh, 2015: 35, [my italics]). In contemporary fiction such as Aminatta Forna's *Happiness* (2019), there is the enrichment of multi-cultural narratives, an artful exploration of identity, relationship and role across different countries. I am drawn to fiction that weaves together past and present political and historical realities. These include *The Kite Runner* by Khaled Hossieni (2003) and *The Inheritance of Loss* by Kiran Desai (2006). I have been struck by the ubiquity of grief as a theme, as well as the skill of writing that enables us to feel the creative tension between despair and hope in human life amidst the complexity of a globalised world. Meera Syal's *The Hidden Mothers* (2015), for example, captures the comedy and pain of transnational surrogacy, whilst Donal Ryan's *From a Low and Quiet Sea* (2018) intertwines the story of a Syrian refugee with two Irish locals, John and Lampy, leading very different lives. I like to think of the kinship between writers and hundreds of thousands of readers, sharing the labour of witnessing our larger tribe in its tribulations and joys.

Chimananda Ngosi Adichie warns us of the need to challenge the colonial legacy that permeates Western culture's creation of stereotypes: 'They make one story become the only story' (Adichie, 2009). This may be why I am reluctant to single out particular books here as a self-supervisory 'aid' for a particular client or situation. For it is in the very complexity of each work of fiction that we are not merely informed but changed at multiple perceptual levels. Good fiction often apprehends and articulates what may be at the edge in terms of racial, cultural or climate consciousness – for example, *The Year of the Runaways* (Sahota, 2015) or *The Overstory* (Powers, 2018). It feeds back into clinical work through bringing home (into my embodied understanding) multi-layered dimensions of transcultural and transgenerational stories. This means that whether it be an Irish client, a Syrian refugee, or a Black British lesbian, I have some familiarity with a wider context that I can draw on to inform my empathy.

Reading (or as I prefer now, listening to audiobooks) nourishes and refreshes the very processes that are intrinsic to our work. Literary critic Waugh proposes that '[t]he novel might be considered the most effective instrument the modern world has evolved for exercising all aspects of the "social brain"' (2015: 58). In addition, research shows that reading puts our brains into a pleasurable trance-like state, similar to meditation, and it brings the same health benefits of deep relaxation and inner calm (Seiter, 2018).

Ballet and Contemporary Dance: Enhancing Musicality and Core Rhythmicity

Where reading supports mentalising, dancing develops expressivity. We move from receptivity to active embodiment. Each clinician needs to have their own ways of releasing the accumulated effects and affects of their work, restoring their sense of vitality and rejuvenating the pleasure of being a body. For me, dance reliably restores a sense of joyfulness, exuberance, passion and flow.

Amber Gray, a DMP who specialises in international trauma work, writes about the importance of 'core rhythmicity':

> Oscillations of rhythms, especially when they are reinforced by externally changing tempos (i.e. with different types of music), can provide a feed-back loop to core [biological] rhythms of the human body (…). Rhythm regulates physiological and emotional responses restoring the capacity for transitions between states of pleasurable arousal and recuperative rest.
>
> (Gray, 2018: 211–12)

My original training is in Body Psychotherapy and in recent years I have sought to develop the skills that are part of a DMP curriculum. Ballet was my first love, followed by contemporary dance, which incorporates aspects of non-Western dance, and I have returned to classes in both these. Having already worked as a therapist for 25 years, I appreciate how dance enhances kinaesthetic and proprioceptive awareness which underpins spatial-relational skills and attunement. These include strengthening the sense of a mid-line, a frame, ground, balance, and confident orientation in three hundred sixty degree space. The rapid coordination of legs, arms, head, feet, hands and eyes builds whole body interconnectivity and aliveness.

This in turn supports the development of embodied reflexivity by challenging me to hold awareness of multiple foci of movement, position, rhythm, coordination and articulation and *at the same time* to surrender to the music, allowing the flow of feeling and relating in space and to other dancers. I enjoy the variation of multiple cultural music traditions and the range of evocative symphonic music used in ballet. This, combined with the artistry of dance vocabulary, and synchronising with others, invites bonding at a deep non-verbal level. Musicality is a form of participative empathy in the vast palette of human emotional experience (Malloch & Trevarthen, 2009). It heightens our capacity to embody empathy and shift fluidly between different emotional states.

Dance class is not a place to think about clients and their stories but to re-claim and refine my sense of embodied ownership and expressive agency. As therapists we are often resonating with clients' suffering in harsh gendered, racial and sociopolitical realities. To remain refreshed and resilient for clients, I need an outlet. Ballet can transport me to a world of lightness and grace, of jumps and turns and lyrical flow. Afro-Caribbean dance is more earth-oriented, inviting a flexible torso and spine, articulated pelvis and isolation of the limbs. This gives me excitement and empowerment grounded in polyrhythmic beats and movements. Currently I attend classes online and feel the difference from being in the studio. I miss the shared movement, the momentum of moving in a bigger space and the felt resonance of the music in that space. It underlines for me how crucial these aspects are.

The Holding Circle: Authentic Movement

The Discipline of Authentic Movement derives originally from the work of the pioneering dance therapist Mary Whitehouse. Her student Janet Adler took Jung's idea of the collective unconscious and framed Authentic Movement as a practice which can support and develop conscious embodiment of the collective. 'The collective body', she wrote is 'the body-felt connectedness among people' (1994: 192). Adler suggests that the loss of community, of the 'sacred circle' (…) [has] contributed significantly to the creation of unbearable rage, isolation and despair' and that our longing for a shift in consciousness 'must be an embodied shift (…). One by one (…) knowing in our bodies that we belong, creates a collective body in which life energy is shared' (ibid).

Since 1994 I have studied Authentic Movement with Linda Hartley and have been a regular participant in her annual retreats. Through very refined and detailed guidance, Linda holds and transmits the developmental potential of Authentic Movement (Hartley, 2004). She has facilitated and sustained a broad community of movers over decades. The kind of deep containment that comes from 'the circle' in Authentic Movement is nourished by the consistency with which its principles are honoured in her teaching. As I reflect on what supports my self-supervision, I am aware that these Authentic Movement groups have formed the crucible for deep internal work, as well as the practice of witnessing skills (Carroll, 2015).

Authentic Movement is defined by the alternation of mover and witness roles. The circle begins with silent eye contact between witnesses and movers. A chime bar is struck and then the movers close their eyes, turn their attention inward and wait to be moved. The holding field of those who witness is receptive and steady. The movers, with eyes closed to the external world, trace clues from their inner world, feeling into the unknown. Each listens for a sensation or an image and follows this; then pauses perhaps, waiting for the next unfolding impulse. Sometimes movers come into contact, interacting in an emergent process. Viewed as a group practice, it often features extraordinary synchronous events as movers' gestures and stories coincide and converge in the intersubjective field.

Afterwards each mover tracks her experience in words, aiming to stay close to the phenomenological detail. In response, the witness succinctly shares her perceptions, owning the subjectivity of her experience through phrases like 'I saw...', 'I felt...', 'I heard...'. For Adler, Authentic Movement is as much about the witness's longing to see clearly, as the mover's desire to be seen. The witnessing capacity develops over time in conscious commitment to oneself and to the other. This skill lends itself to self-supervision (Payne, 2001) but it is also different. In Authentic Movement, evaluation is suspended in order for the space to be truly open.

In the group facilitated by Linda Hartley over many years, I have found a great freedom of possibilities and interactions. Playful contact, tender touch, or push and pull, bring tactile enquiry to the fore. The level of sensitivity and connectedness between movers enables heightened communication and co-creation. Bodies pile up in strange configurations. Several movers might slither over the floor, while another pair clings together or moves sensuously. Or sounding builds momentum, with percussive interventions, chorus and counterpoint. Sometimes we howl like 'witches', with movements to match the hiss and crackle. I find a profound catharsis in this: a renewal through immersion in 'a sense of something ancient, forgotten and vital' (MacMahon, 2015: 363). This wildness is still contained by internal and external witnessing, however, and is followed by the sequential tracking and weaving of narrative threads with the embodied haiku-like economy. It is full of surprises and synchronicities that reveal multiple stories and archetypal themes.

After more than 20 years of Authentic Movement practice, I am experiencing a shift in my movement process. As if opening a new door, I sometimes step into what feels like a live three-dimensional story in which I am a participant. These scenes are rich with associations to myth, culture and the collective rather than personal memories. I have found myself living out effects and stories which, like dreams, are vivid and extraordinary. They do not feel 'mine', nor is it like conscious story making but rather I am being moved in ways which are emergent and spontaneous.

In 2015, I wrote a long article called 'The Blood-dimmed Tide: Witnessing War and the Collective Body in Authentic Movement' which was a record of my movement process in two groups over the period of a year. It began with this powerful experience, in a peer group hosted by Heba Zaphiriou-Zarifi,

> I enter the circle carrying a cushion and a blanket. I feel fragile. Burrowing down under the blanket brings a feeling of being hurt and little. I start to rub the blanket between my hands and find I am suddenly wrestling with it. Something is happening; a violent struggle; a doer and a done-to. I am fighting to survive. Yelling, clawing, kicking.
>
> I am on my back now. I feel my spine on the floor. I start to snake my hips, feeling with pleasure the friction between my back and the carpet. My whole body sings. I feel sensual, powerful, coiling and uncoiling. But then suddenly I am kicking, shouting, arching my back off the floor, raging, raging. I am rolling, squirming, arms and legs pushing, then still. One long scream, tears streaming down, helpless fury.
>
> I lie on my back for a long, long time. I keep my hands cupped over my eye sockets. I am in limbo. I cannot look, I cannot see, I must not. I am stunned. I am shamed.

(Carroll, 2015: 197)[3]

Whilst Authentic Movement is often used as a supervision tool, this was not the purpose of this group. However, it immediately struck me that I was currently seeing four clients who were bringing their experience of being sexually abused as children. That very week, painful, explicit details in the narrative of their abuse had emerged. It brought home to me how their ongoing shock, fear, rage, confusion and shame were still reverberating in me. To find I had unwittingly enacted the complexity and intensity of my resonating response was both a relief (I felt contained by the circle) and an education.

Yet this was only the starting point of my movement. I continued:

> Something compels me to get on my feet. Without moving my hands from my face, I find a way to crouch. There is a crowd around me. I feel an unfamiliar desire. A desire to menace. It is so clear, so powerful, so precise. I want to intimidate, threaten, accuse ...
>
> Everyone. Everywhere around me there is violence, bloodshed, rape. And there is a crowd of onlookers. My eyes remain closed, my hands are still over my eyes and my hair is over my hands. I stand, and through these shields I stare. I stare methodically, progressing round the circle so each person will feel my stare, my accusation.
>
> I move further into the circle. My hands drop and fold together at my lap. I lift a sword, a big heavy sword. I lift it up to threaten, intimidate, and

menace those around me. I have never known such ugly brutal power. I am fearless amidst the violence. I feel poised for revenge, capable of harming. But also, witnessing myself still, I question myself. What am I doing with this malevolent power? Why am I holding onto it? I am aware of my female witnesses, and the palpable sense of the circle holding me. What must I do?

The answer comes from an inner voice which says: "Turn it around." I take it to mean I must transform this hatred, not re-enact it. And so, I start to circle the sword, still gripped by both hands, above my head.

Suddenly the sword is turning to decapitate me, and with a scream I fall to my knees. Shock and terror shake my body as I collapse on the floor. I know the sequence is over. I know I have survived. I feel relief and a devastating sense of impotence. Did I think I could choose?

Other movers gather to rock and soothe me. I am a child again, being comforted by women.

(ibid)

The immediate consequence of this movement experience on me was an acute sense of humankind's collective failure as bystanders to the trauma of all kinds. Why do we not act to protect others from harm? It was a question which seemed to come from a horrified innocence and a genuine bewilderment. These experiences prompted intense reflection in me on the impact of hearing constant news of war and sexual violence (and seeing it in films), as well as processing these themes in clinical work. This period was marked by escalating violence in the Middle East, in particular the civil war in Syria, which resulted in displacement and horrendous loss suffered by many. Reference to beheadings in the news had had an especially visceral impact. This was trauma history on a world scale, and I recognised that the West as a colonial perpetrator had played – and plays – its part in this.

In subsequent months, I came again and again to embody positions on the victim-perpetrator continuum, with violent acts and death as the constant organising theme and fulcrum. I felt pulled into the underworld. What was useful and humbling to me was the vivid sense of stepping fully into dissociated parts of myself and others. As part of self-supervision of my own clinical work, one of the meanings I took from this sequence was the need to find and work more rigorously with the perpetrator in myself, in colonial power structures and the (internalised) perpetrator states in my clients, and also to pay attention to – and invite exploration of – the effect of news and film on my clients as well.

Adorisio suggests that through Authentic Movement we can sense the multidimensional character of every facet of reality (2007), and that 'the fluid movement between the polarities allows for the discovery of right distance, the avoidance of crystallising positions and the opening of a space for transformation' (ibid: 95). This encapsulates what I have found in these groups and what I explore at length in my discussion of witnessing war and the collective body (Carroll, 2015; Blend & Carroll, 2020). In a reflection on one such group, MacMahon writes of the sense of 'collective participation (…) in a very prescient and urgent ritual' (2015: 361).

Self-supervision includes asking the bigger questions about the nature of the work we do and how it is evolving. Critically, it means thinking about how we respond to an escalating sense of a world in crisis, as we see even more sharply now in Covid times, as embodied community and human contact are jeopardised.

In these processes I include under the umbrella of self-supervision, I seek to digest the impact of each clinical encounter and also the world I am part of, the collective. I attempt to recognise what is stirred, know it more deeply and have perspective when the default might easily be to carry it in tightness, anxiety or dissociation. Self-supervision means I take responsibility for my reflexivity. But what actually holds me is *community* via Authentic Movement, talking with colleagues, dance classes and reading, the arts or other forms of participation such as being outdoors in the collective of nature.

The semi-structured network of therapy – with clients, therapists, supervisors, trainers and supervisors of supervisors in multi-situated positions – does support resilience, flexibility, turn-taking and creativity. It is remarkable, really: the holding of space to process and the way this is passed on, and handed back, in a ritual which is as old as the circle around the fire and as contemporary as its continuation now in many settings and contexts. As Adler suggests: 'new energy repeatedly, cyclically, accrues from life (…) is gathered, contained, dispersed back into the collective through one body, then another, then another' (1994: 206).

Notes

1 Warm thanks to Penny Best and Sissy Lykou for their feedback on this chapter and to Mark Kelly for lively conversation about dance and psychotherapy, and the links between them.
2 My gratitude goes to Shoshi Asheri (2013) with whom I taught Integrative Relational Psychotherapy at The Minster Centre (2007–20). I learned so much from and with her especially concerning fluidity and rigour as we developed the concept of 'embodied reflexivity' in our clinical work and teaching.
3 Reproduced with kind permission from John Wiley & Sons, Ltd Copyright © 2015.

References

Adichie, C. N. (2009). The Danger of a Single Story. *TED talk*. October 9. www.ted.com/talks/chimamanda_ngozi_adichie_the_danger_of_a_single_story?language=en
Adler, J. (1994). The collective body. In P. Pallaro (Ed.) *Authentic Movement: Essays by Mary Starks Whitehouse, Janet Adler and Joan Chodorow*. London: Jessica Kingsley Publishers. 190–208.

Adorisio, A. (2007). Moving towards complexity: the myth of Echo and Narcissus. In P. Pallaro (Ed.) *Authentic Movement: Moving the Body, Moving the Self, Being Moved.* London, UK: Jessica Kingsley Publishers. 80–96.

Asheri & Carroll (2015). Humanising the therapeutic relationship: the transformative power and risk of 'Felt Participation'. *Advances in Relational Psychotherapy. Confer online module.* Recorded 15 July 2015. www.confer.uk.com/module/module-relatio nal.html

Asheri, S. (2013). Stepping into the void of dissociation: a therapist and client in search of a meeting place. In J. Yellin & O. Badouk Epstein (Eds.) *Terror Within and Without, Attachment and Disintegration: Working on the Edge.* London: Karnac. 73–89.

Best, P. (2008). 'Interactive reflections: moving between modes of expression as a model for supervision. In H. Payne (Ed.) *Supervision of Dance Movement Psychotherapy.* London: Routledge. 137–53.

Blend, J. & Carroll, R. (2020). Witnessed improvised diaspora journey enactments (widje): an experiential method for exploring refugee history. *Jewish Historical Studies.* 51(1): 246–66.

Butté, C. & Evertsen, L. (2020). Editorial: special issue on migration. *Body, Movement and Dance in Psychotherapy,* 15(2): 133–41. DOI: 10.1080 17432979.2020. 1784685

Carroll, R. (2021). Editorial: embodied intersubjectivity as online psychotherapy becomes mainstream. *Body, Movement and Dance in Psychotherapy.* 16(1) 1–8 DOI: 10.1080 17432979.2021.1883402

Carroll, R. (2020). Future flat-packed or future fluid: why normal is the problem. In R. Carroll & J. Ryan (Eds.) *What is Normal? Psychotherapists Explore the Question.* London: Confer Publications. 147–56.

Carroll, R. (2015). The blood-dimmed tide: witnessing war and working with the collective body in authentic movement. *Journal of Psychotherapy and Politics International.* 13(3) 194–208. DOI: 10.1002/ppi.1360

Deleuze, G. (1969). *The Logic of Sense,* translated by M. Lester & C. Stivale and edited by C. V. Boundas. New York: Columbia University Press.

Desai, K. (2006/2008). *The Inheritance of Loss* [Audiobook]. Narrated by Rodrigues, T. www.audible.co.uk/pd/The-Inheritance-of-Loss-Audiobook/004FTZRTG

Duncan, R. (2018). *Nature in Mind: Systemic Thinking and Imagination in Ecopsychology and Mental Health.* Abingdon: Routledge.

Evaristo, B. (2019). *Girl, Woman, Other.* London: Penguin.

Forna, A. (2019). *Happiness* [Audiobook]. Narrated by Miles, R. www.audible.co.uk/ pd/Happiness-Audiobook/B07C42X3PY

Gray, A. (2018). Roots, rhythm, reciprocity. In S. W. Porges & D. Dana, *Clinical Applications of the Polyvagal theory; the emergence of polyvagal-informed therapies.* New York: Norton. 207–27.

Hartley, L. (2004). *Somatic Psychology: Body, Mind and Meaning.* London: Whurr.

Hossieni, K. (2003). *The Kite Runner.* London: Riverhead books.

Jordan, M. (2014). *Nature and Therapy: Understanding Counselling and Psychotherapy in Outdoor Spaces.* Abingdon: Routledge.

Lorde, A. (1988). *A Burst of Light and Other Essays.* Ithaca, NY: Firebrand books.

lykou, s. (2021). Sociopolitical perspectives on trauma in a world in crisis: the personal is political revisited. In s. lykou & A. Chesner (Eds.) *Trauma in the Creative and Embodied Therapies: When Words Are Not Enough.* Abingdon: Routledge.

Malloch, S. & Trevarthen, C. (Eds.) (2009). *Communicative Musicality: Exploring the Basis of Human Companionship*. Oxford: Oxford Press.

MacMahon, S. (2015). Holy Dreaming – poetry and movement. *Journal of Dance & Somatic Practice*, 7(2): 359–63. DOI: 10.1386/jdsp.7.2.359_1

Payne, H. (2001). Authentic movement and supervision. *e-motion. ADMT.UK Newsletter*, 13(4): 4–7.

Powers, R. (2018). *The Overstory*. New York: W. W. Norton.

Reeve, S. (2008). Ecological Movement. Extract from Unpublished PhD Thesis. www.moveintolife.com/thesis-ecological-movement.html

Reeve, S. (2011). *Nine Ways of Seeing a Body*. Axminster: Triarchy Press.

Ryan, D. (2018). *From a Low and Quiet Sea*. New York: Doubleday.

Sahota, S. (2015). *The Year of the Runaways* [Audiobook]. Narrated by Garewal, S. www.audible.co.uk/pd/The-Year-of-the-Runaways-Audiobook/B015JMGFDO

Seiter, C. (2018). The surprising power of reading fiction: 9 ways it makes us happier and more creative. [Weblog]. *Buffer*. April 19. https://open.buffer.com/reading-fiction/

Syal, M. (2015). *The Hidden Mothers*. New York: Doubleday.

The Free Dictionary (n.d.), retrieved October 11th 2020 from www.thefreedictionary.com/debacles

Waugh, P. (2015). The novel as therapy: Ministrations of voice in an age of risk. *Journal of the British Academy*, 3: 35–68. DOI: 10.5871/jba/003.035

Chapter 9

Holding Sacred

The Woman's Body in Supervision

*Annette Schwalbe, Sue Curtis and
Christina Greenland*

Introduction

This chapter presents a way of being with each other in supervision that serves the woman therapist and her woman clients to recover trust, presence and joy in their bodies. It aims to convey relational tones and themes that intertwine along the line that connects supervisor of supervisor – supervisor – therapist and client.

At the centre of this chapter rests the body of a woman. A body that came into being, grew and developed in a world that still considers women as less than men, or as too much. A body that knows, historically and presently, collectively and individually, the potential or the experience of being objectified or violated. A body that, in places, has become timid, fearful and often unable to make itself felt and heard in life, therapy and also supervision. Her body, the body of a woman with breasts and without, with womb and without, with menstrual blood flowing or not, with labia and clitoris or not. Body of a grandmother, body of a mother, body of a daughter, body of a sister, body of a friend, or body of a lover (Figure 9.1).

It is important to recognise that the experience of being a woman is not universal. There are, for example, ways of being a woman that do not depend on having a body that was assigned female at birth. Having a body assigned female also does not necessarily make one identify as a woman. Nor does a woman necessarily perform all or any of the roles mentioned above. Experiences of womanhood are influenced by social, cultural, political, religious and geographical factors, among others.

It is acknowledged that this chapter is written by three white, Western and cisgender women, assigned female at birth and identifying as women. It is this particular combination with its particular herstory and limitations that informs this chapter's approach to the woman's body whilst knowing that there is more. It neither attempts to speak for all women nor exclude anyone who finds this text relevant to their experience.

The three co-authors speak to their own and each other's bodies in their supervision encounters and supervisory relationships over time. In their

DOI: 10.4324/9781003034940-10

Figure 9.1 Holding sacred the woman's body.

roles as supervisor of supervisor, supervisor and supervisee, they identify key aspects of their supervision experience that hold sacred their embodied presence as woman practitioners and enable the client to heal her embodied wounds.

Far from being a purely academic exercise, the writing of this chapter is based on a ritual and creative research process. It includes various forms of personal and visceral storytelling that convey the sacred nature of the subject matter at hand. Most importantly, it has come onto the page by taking turns, one woman's words inspiring another woman's writing. The resulting text is born of an ongoing relationship.

The Three Co-authors

Sue

As I begin this writing in April 2020, I am in a 12-week lockdown in response to the Covid-19 pandemic. I have been placed in the UK governments 'at risk' and vulnerable group due to health considerations. The invisible virus outside reminds me of the invisible cancer cells that 10 years ago lived in my blood and wreaked havoc in my peripheral nerves leaving me disabled. Now, 10 years later, I am recovering from bilateral breast cancer and awaiting radiotherapy – another treatment that will invade my tissues.

Figure 9.2 Sue.

My body knows loss and grief at the depths of my being. I am in my sixties, post-menopausal and lived through two miscarriages and the emotional pain of lives unlived. The grief touches a place that has been present in my own body's formation in the womb and resonates at the core of my 30 years of supervision practice. Mid pregnancy with me my mother's mother passed away, and I have always sensed the loss. When I was born, her milk did not sustain me, and unable to 'thrive'. I was bottle-fed. The sense of struggle to receive and nurture during an embryonic process and post birth is deeply embedded, and I have come to trust my body's searching with all my senses the 'unformed' mystery of bringing to life.

I love supervising trainees and newly graduated therapists, to touch and be alongside the embryonic stage of practice, tending to, like a gardener, the unseen seeds and bulbs within the soil and having the privilege of witnessing early growth and later blossoming (Figure 9.2).

I remember my first encounters with Annette as she entered the Dance Movement Psychotherapy training, as her tutor and supervisor. She had a vibrancy, vitality and deep care for the world and her peers that opened spaces of reflection. I was fascinated and moved by her stories from around the world and her cultural sensitivity. Once she had qualified, I was honoured to continue supervising her work across countries and witness the development of her somatic body mapping work, where the body's innermost, raw experience is moved, revealed and manifest in a visual life-size map (Schwalbe, 2019). Fifteen years later when I got cancer, she guided me through my own body map that spanned five years of illness to recovery and that I presented at an exhibition she organised entitled 'Seasons of a Woman' (2015). Today, I still supervise Annette's supervisory practice.

I met Christina on a somatic body mapping weekend whilst working on my own map. Eyes closed and lost within my own body sensations I heard the sound of scratching; rhythmic, subtle and continuous. My body was exploring again being in the depths of the earth, my known place of not fully formed and the gentle scratching sounds surrounding me felt like an archaeologist gently scraping away the earth to find me. Upon re-entry to the conscious space, I found Christina laying hidden underneath her body map quietly scratching its unseen side.

This memory is deeply imprinted within me, bringing to life symbolically the place I hold sacred in supervision; the unseen and unformed depths. Whilst delighting with supervisees who have gone on to birth their own children, it has also been vital in supervision to explore with those who, like myself, have little ones who breathe elsewhere.

Annette

I am a dance movement psychotherapist in menopause, nearing the end of my 40s. My supervisory practice started 20 years ago when I was living in Pakistan with my husband and was pregnant with our first child. I was assisting a psychiatrist and psychotherapist from Islamabad in weekly group supervision at a local organisation supporting women and children who were experiencing domestic and institutional violence. My role was to add a body perspective to the therapeutic work discussed.

My own body was with a child at that time, and so was one of the psychotherapists in the group. In supervision, this was cherished and thought about. As her baby grew, however, and her bump started to show she had to stop facilitating a psycho-educational group with members of the police force. In this context, the sight of her pregnant body – evidence of her being a sexually active woman – was deemed offensive by the policemen. With limited cultural scope to challenge this openly, my colleague returned to the back office where, in time, she set up a crib for her child, then a playpen. Throughout, she continued to work in various capacities as psychotherapist, with her early motherhood and changing body, however, often held a secret.

My own path was different, leading my family to live in Uganda shortly after giving birth. Here, I became part of a wider as well as professional culture that openly referenced the sexual body and honoured the mothering body of a woman. Working as a lecturer and clinical supervisor at the university, I was able to breastfeed during meetings and later bring my toddling daughter into class. When I got pregnant again, I was treated with awe by colleagues and supervisees who insisted on carrying my bags across campus in order to protect mother and unborn child.

Figure 9.3 Annette.

Throughout those years, I received supervision on the phone from Sue who had continued to supervise me after the end of my training in the UK. I remember vividly the time when, between the birth of my first and second child, I lost a third through an early miscarriage. In supervision, this was attended to by Sue with great care and understanding of how this was temporarily affecting my trust in my embodied ability to hold clients, students and supervisees.

These experiences have shaped the way I supervise today and endeavour to hold safe and sacred, but not secret, my own and the bodies of woman supervisees. The visible and invisible life that we have, kindle, hold, give, lose and renew in and through our bodies, whether childbearing and child-raising or not (Figure 9.3).

That this renewal doesn't just happen in and through one woman's body but also in community and lineage became clear to me when I met Christina, first as a trainee client and then as a supervisee and somatic body mapping colleague. I remember sitting together in my studio, witnessing her gentle self-touch in service of psychic exploration and appreciating her profound courage to come up close with raw and tender experiences in herself and others. Suddenly, a deep knowing of professional passage surfaced and rejoiced in me. Nurtured over so many years by Sue's example of loving, long-standing and deeply committed supervisory relationships with me and many others, I recognised Christina as one next in line and remember clearly thinking: 'it's your turn now!'

Christina

I have practiced as a Dance Movement Psychotherapist in NHS secondary mental health services since qualifying four years ago. Annette was my therapist during training and, after a break of two years, became my supervisor. We have always remained conscious and taken great care over the transitions and multi-dimensions in our relationship which now also includes being colleagues.

While it is uncommon to move from a client/therapist to a supervisee / supervisor relationship, I found it very beneficial. I appreciate our shared understanding of my personal story including points of comfort and discomfort, strengths and struggles that are inevitably sparked by the experiences my clients bring to therapy. I also value the trust between us that continues to deepen through the supervisee /supervisor relationship. As Annette became my supervisor and I began to know her differently, less idealised, we openly named those changes.

It was in Annette's presence that I first experienced moving before a witness. There I stood, a little shy to be moving in front of another. I felt her body before me and heard her steady voice, like an anchor in these strange new waters. Gradually, I became emboldened and soon found that my body had a voice and was compelled to speak. It spoke words that I had not carefully chosen to lay before a stranger. They were powerful, unexpected and exhilarating. After moving, in that moment of stillness, when the orchestra ceases and the silence resonates, I opened my eyes. And there I saw my blue-grey-eyed audience, Annette. But she was no casual observer, she had travelled with me and now her gaze met mine, unflinching and utterly alive.

Over the years we have worked together, in the many different iterations of our relationship, her way of seeing has become so familiar to me. It is not, however, something I take for granted. Time and again, I have emerged from some movement exploration, be it painful or playful, frightening or joyous, to be greeted by her compassionate, fearless witnessing. It is in this supervision space, where all is welcome, that I have endeavoured to bring my whole self to the service of my clients, allowing their stories to collide with mine, to echo in my body and so be seen and known.

I work with women for whom it has not been easy or possible to feel safety, love or pleasure in their bodies, and this can touch on aspects of my own life. However, I have also known much love, sensual and sexual delight and enjoyed the sounds, shape and rhythm of my body. At forty, it is a place I can call home. In supervision, I continue to explore and relish the pleasures of my sensory realm. I have learned not to see this as frivolous or self-indulgent but as a way of familiarising myself with my bodily landscape and holding it sacred so that, with authenticity, I can invite my clients to explore theirs (Figure 9.4).

Figure 9.4 Christina.

My memory of meeting Sue on a somatic body mapping retreat resonates with this joyfulness. I see her standing in front of her body map singing at the top of her voice, paintbrush in hand, smiling. Her energy was infectious and soon I too was singing with gusto. Since then, we have become collective body mapping colleagues and I have immense respect for her humour, kindness and wisdom. Together, Annette and Sue form part of a strong ancestry of women in the profession from its birth to the present that allows me to feel affirmed, assured and proud.

Holding Sacred the Woman's Body: A Collective Body Mapping Ritual as Artistic Enquiry

In September 2019, the three of us came together to explore further how we hold sacred the woman's body in supervision. 'Holding sacred' in this context we define as both an attitude and an act. As an attitude, it is based on a belief in something bigger and deeper than us individually and collectively, and beyond the human form. This is linked to an appreciation of the individual and collective unconscious as conceptualised by C.G. Jung (1968) and fleshed out in somatic terms by Jungian woman scholars, mystics and dance movement psychotherapists such as Marion Woodman (2008), Janet Adler

(2002), Joan Chodorow (2015), Jill Hayes (2013) and Tina Stromsted (2014). Love comes into it as an orienting towards heartfelt connection and a quality of cherishing the other. So does the recognition of an innate life force that orients towards growth and healing. All this combines what shamanic practitioner and dance movement psychotherapist Megan N. Ramos (2018) coined

> a sacred holding environment based in spirit rather than personality ... whereby both parties are able to engage in a sense of allowing and surrender, and whereby natural intelligence of body and spirit guides the unfolding of the healing process and the therapeutic interaction.
>
> (75)

In order to explore what such a sacred holding environment might look like enacted, sound like when articulated in the context of supervision and serve in the work with clients, we decided to engage in a process of artistic enquiry. This is defined by McNiff as a process of 'knowing through the arts' ((2008: 31) that counter-acts a tendency of 'clinification' (Brown, 2008: 202) which under-values and marginalises the meaning that emanates from creative expression, in this case body movement. To instead bring the creative and knowing body centre stage, we chose to perform a Collective Body Mapping Ritual (CBMR). This is a form that we have been developing outside of supervision with a group of colleague therapists and artists since 2015.

At the centre of the CBMR is a large round canvas on which a group of people come together. Through a series of ritual rounds, participants attend to body sensations, trace each other's bodies on the canvas, honour them with creative markings and playfully engage with the co-created bodily landscape. Natural and evocative materials that are specific to the site and occasion of the ritual are used to make tangible and visible the context in which our bodies come into shape and shape each other. Witnessing and speaking during the ritual is formalised and informed by the practice of Authentic Movement with a focus on here-and-now experience and essential, non-interpretive wording (Adler, 2002). In the past, the CBMR has served as a participatory performance in public health and arts-related spaces, as contemplative offering at academic conferences and as a group process in retreat settings. (Schwalbe, Greenland, Curtis & Best, 2017a, Schwalbe, 2017b).

In order to engage with the CBMR as an artistic enquiry for this book chapter, we gathered diverse material: not just thoughts and themes but also things that we could touch, hold, hear, smell, taste and pass to each other, thereby 'weaving webs between discourse and matter' (Frizell 2020: 2). We chose materials that inspired multiple associations – mundane and mythical – with a woman's body and our lives as supervising and supervised practitioners: soil that had composted in Sue's garden for many seasons, beetroot juice that was intended to be slowly cooked in Christina's kitchen but was quickly bought in the supermarket; apples, fallen or picked from the tree in

Figure 9.5 Preparing the ground.

front of Annette's therapy and supervision studio; sways of delicately trans-
lucent as well as stiffened white fabric; hydrangea flower heads, their colours
turning; bulbs with dried-up roots and emerging shoots.

The day we brought it all together and into motion (Figures 9.5–9.10)
we were joined by two colleagues, artist Emma Scott and dance movement
psychotherapist Hannah Murdoch-Payne, who accompanied the ritual as
witnessing photographer and scribe, respectively. Their seeing and hearing
presence further added to the field of embodied knowing that we stepped into.

Three Acts and Articulations of a Woman's Body Holding and Held Sacred in Supervision

The following enactment from the CBMR invokes and evokes the body that
nurtures embryonic states of knowing in supervision.

> *My fingers roll bulbs onto the map and I place one within my belly button,
> sensing its weight deep within this tiny crevice of my body, extending down-
> wards like an umbilical cord. The smell of beetroot juice pervades me as
> I lie at the edge of the map underneath the fine gauze cloth. It's draping
> folds lightly touch my skin and I feel veiled and encased as if in my own,
> lone, amniotic sac. Hannah notes "is she in or is she out?" I am neither and*

Figure 9.6 Gathering material.

Figure 9.7 Tracing each other.

Figure 9.8 Honouring our bodies.

Figure 9.9 Exploring and playing.

Figure 9.10 Marking the co-created bodyscape.

I am both. I wait, gaze, feel and sense. I am embryonic, forming, allowing, noticing the quiet within and just being (Figure 9.11).

As I gaze outwards from my 'edge' place at the vitality and symbols of creativity before me my body feels silent and still, expectant of the surety that an inner growth is developing and revealing. The words 'inscribed & embryonic' face me. Both words I brought to the map and they intrigue me. I am reminded of my favourite psalm:139 'my frame was not hidden from you, when I was being made in secret, intricately wrought in the depths of the earth. Your eyes beheld my unformed substance;' (570 verses 15–16).

Sometime later and not quite sure what inner urge calls me forth, I emerge, crawling then standing, attentive to my body's emotional curiosity at what lies before me. Stepping into the map I place apples as breasts and a hydrangea as a womb on Annette's outline and drip beetroot juice like blood from the vagina of Christina's outline, watching it trickle down the outline of her thighs. I am captivated and entranced by my own delight in their fertility, possibility and nurture. I think of the potential for life, the pain of birth and the grief at babies that never breathed. Celebration and grief intertwine like converging streams, coursing through my veins in a fleeting moment of time; known, felt and marked within.

Journeying on I meet Christina who picks up one of the apple breasts gesturing it towards her mouth. Her eyes widen like a mischievous child and we giggle together as she bites into it (Figure 9.12).

Figure 9.11 Sacred Act One: The Fertilising Body (Sue).

Figure 9.12 Biting into flesh.

I laugh deeply from a child-like place within me, like she has dared to break through some ancient Taboo. Yet at the same time I marvel at her courage to bite deeply into its flesh, grateful for her sensual womanhood that so confidently takes her feed!

I notice how different it is from the shame and humiliation I experienced during my own puberty and navigating my changing body and budding breasts.

I move on through the landscape of us three women, aware at times of my own stumbling, disabled feet, my ageing woman's body and feeling like a grandmother among the generations of women that follow. The sensory landscape of soil, bulbs, flowers and beetroot juice articulating and bringing to life our ongoing trust in each other and the revealing exploration.

I return to my edge place and read again my two words – 'inscribed & embryonic'. They resonate with a known place I experience as a supervisor – beholding and holding sacred developing and unfolding material deep within my supervisee. An embryonic offering or seed, planted within our relationship and one which requires time to ripen.

In supervision I have learned to trust the unformed stirrings within my supervisees, to search, listen and wait when they have no words or struggle to bring forth clear thoughts, images or words. To hold their fears, anxieties and sometimes shame at not 'knowing' in a form they think is expected. Yet it is within this deeply muddy earth that we thrive, and I offer a supervision womb in which they can implant and grow. They are inscribed within me, embedded, embryonic and unfolding as, together with their client's stories they form, shape and emerge.

I remember my own analyst's words 'you don't know what you know!' I now know that 'I know' in a sensory landscape and my role as supervisor is to facilitate supervisees to 'know what they know' and how they know it. As a supervisor my body is expectant and on sacred ground as I watch and wait for what feels like a small baby, supervisee heel to gently push against its amniotic sac, imprinting itself into my supervisor womb.

The following enactment of the CBMR follows the body that *reclaims violated aspects of being in supervision* (Figure 9.13).

We play with the beetroot juice still pooling on the paper. I am standing and pausing for a moment when Sue dips her brush into the deep red and starts to paint my toenails. I delight in the attention, then my feelings change: the juice seeps into the skin of my toes and leaves them red-rimmed. They now look bloodied, like tortured feet.

I think of the ballet dancer and high-heeled woman, elevated to an icon to be consumed. I think of broken and bound feet of women in some cultures of the past, reduced to an ideal to be controlled.

Figure 9.13 Sacred Act Two: The Renewing Body (Annette).

I start to trace on the ground with my oozing toes and, without intent, leave a mark that looks like the face of a ghost. I let it be. For now. I move on, don't speak of it. Not yet. Instead, not far from this place of body-less presence on the map I see Christina laying soil on the ground in front of a note pinned to apple: 'to behold' it says.

All three of us are now engaged in bringing different things to this place that starts to look like an altar: more soil, more apples, bulbs, a hydrangea flower head. I think of the client who we serve in supervision. The client, who on this map, does not have a solid body outline. However, her altar is here. She is all ingredients whilst she remains unseen, untouched, unnamed in her full form.

As my gaze wanders, I see another note: 'clinical' it says. I remember having placed this word, with client in mind, into the folds of the gauze-like fabric around the map early on. Clinical practice, clinical supervision, clinical client – a chill runs down my spine. How can she find her feet in such labelled land? How can we call her in during supervision without re-casting her in objectifying terms?

I go back to our place of sacred assembly. This time, I dip the brush into the red juice myself and write around the place: "for you" (Figure 9.14).

We offer, we don't take. We approach her through our own zest and weariness of being women on this earth. We offer a bite from the apple of our

Figure 9.14 For you.

collective truth, offer to help her find a way through the gate so that she
can leave what had been sold to her as paradise. We know that it takes
a different kind of garden to raise her up again, this time in full flesh and
blood. Not abused, not violated, not shamed, not drained.

In supervision, we cultivate what is needed for such renewal and unhin-
dered growth: a shared ability to let the blood flow again, through veins and
body places that are lifeless or in pain. And a willingness by supervisor and
supervisee to bear the pins and needles as the blood flow re-awakens limbs,
gestures and utterings that were lost when she was stopped in her tracks
before. This work of 'body-visory' regeneration is not a job to be completed.
It is ongoing and cyclical as it assists '(...)the birth that is never accomplished,
the body never created once and for all, the form never definitively completed,
the face always still to be formed. The lips never opened or closed on a truth'
(Irigaray, 1985: 217).

The following enactment of the CBMR brings alive the body that *cultivates*
sensory and relational pleasure in supervision (Figure 9.15).

It's your turn. With your eyes half closed you step across our shared land-
scape, exploring it, finding your place. Your body, the way you move, it's
so familiar to me. I'm restful yet curious. Slowly you lower yourself to the

Figure 9.15 Sacred Act Three: The Relishing Body (Christina).

ground. You are close to finding your place from where I will trace your out-
line. It will be my turn next.

You lie down, your long, slender body curves towards Sue's shape, already
traced. Gently, you place your hand, with gold ring finger, over the outline
of hers. This gesture to your teacher, your guide, it feels intimate, respectful.
I imagine wet beetroot under palm. As I see you there, my own teacher, my
guide, I wonder, "will there be space for me?" Then, after a moment, with
your hand still in place, you stretch out and I see there is room for me now.
An internal, grateful sigh escapes me.

You become still but I wait, silently witnessing, respecting your right to
be particular, to change your mind. I hold sacred the wisdom and authority
of your body, as you have held mine, over and over again, so that in time
I learned how to do this for myself. Now I do it for you.

With tenderness and attention, I paint Annette's body outline, working
my way around her contours. The iron, bloodlike smell of the beetroot
accompanies me. I relish the earthy taste in my mouth. I come to her ring
fingered hand that rests over the outline of Sue's hand, as if gaining some
quiet strength from her. Placing my hand over both, and with another sigh,
I join this intimate company of touch (Figure 9.16).

I recognise these little sighs of mine, accompanied by a sense of landing
gently in this world where I am not alone. I remember how we had explored

Figure 9.16 Intimate company of touch.

them in supervision some months ago. That time, we had both sat on the floor and I had closed my eyes to sense my body whilst also lightly holding my clients in my mind: their bodies and experiences of trauma. I knew that whilst I was doing so, Annette was witnessing my movements from her place in the room. Her quiet presence was familiar and reassuring.

I took my hand to touch the contours of my face, gently contacting my skin, tracing what I know to be me. Little sighs escaped my lips, very small sounds. Sounds that I was familiar with from moments of stirring from sleep at night. I attended to how they landed in the space, how they sounded to me, and how I wondered they might sound to Annette, too. For me, they were little moans of sorrow and pleasure in one.

During that supervision session, still sighing intermittently, I turned my hands to the space in front of me as if making contact with my clients who, I imagined, were facing me. My fingers moved gently up and down, as if caressing the tensions in their bodies. After some time, I eased myself into the softness of the cushions behind me and slid down onto the warm, firm ground. My body felt open, without need to defend, and I relished a sense of safety in this room, with Annette. I had a strong sense of her embodied presence, as if it provided a soft landing that breaks my fall into this world and into the world of my clients.

Again, a vision of my clients emerged: that I, in turn, can be the body that provides a soft landing and teaches my clients to slowly relax (back) into life.

Embodied Modes of Holding Sacred in Supervision

The three acts above hold sacred the woman's body in supervision in different ways. Each is informed by the individual nature and life story of the one enacting. Each act also goes beyond personal inclination and touches on collective themes and struggles of embodiment that are specifically, yet not exclusively, relevant to the experience of women. Knowing in body, respectfully naming, and sensitively engaging with these experiences, themes and struggles is crucial for the creation of a sacred holding environment in supervision.

One embodied mode of holding sacred, here articulated as the Fertilising Body, is the sustained and womb-like appreciation of what is subtle, barely perceptible and knowable in supervision. The practice of this appreciation allows both, supervisor and supervisee to hold the supervisee's growing skills and understanding of her work as if it was an embryo that is forming and needs to be nurtured and connected with intuitively and through a bodily felt sense. It is a practice of tending to and keeping fertile the ground from which the supervisee can grow and draw.

The choice of the embryo as a metaphor is not by chance. Menzam-Sills, a scholar and practitioner of pre-and perinatal psychology, describes the significance of early development

> as the embryo folds into a more three-dimensional form, where the heart meets an energetic heart centre and miraculously begins to beat. The little one begins to resemble more of what we are used to considering as a body. I have heard that some spiritual traditions consider this the time when the soul or spirit enters the body. There seems to be more of a body to enter into.
>
> (2020: 448)

It is the heartbeat in the supervisee's forming practice that supervisor and supervisee feel and listen to. That this is not a rational or analytic process but an embodied and heartfelt one is further supported by Appleton who integrates prenatal, transpersonal and somatic psychology. With the embryo biologically forming around its heart as life-sustaining and life-organising centre long before there is a brain, he states, 'the intelligence of the heart is primary to the intelligence of the brain' (2020: 103). To reveal the significance and felt quality of such intelligence, he speaks of this stage of embryonic development as one of 'the embryo dreaming itself into existence', a dreaming that centres around its heart 'as the fulcrum around which form takes shape' (ibid).

Tuning into the intelligence of the embryonic dream, that is, the role of the Fertilising Body in supervision. Or, as Davis puts it in her article that explores the meeting of sacred ritual and psychotherapy: 'We are performing an act of imagination, one that has the possibility of transforming what "is" into "what yet could be"' (2000: 128).

Another mode of holding sacred in supervision, here articulated as the Renewing Body, is the explicit and shared embodied resonance with the collective (historical and contemporary) experience of the violated woman's body. In this context, 'holding sacred' in supervision can be close to 'holding alive'. When exploring phenomena of dissociation in the work with clients who have experienced trauma, McGinty argues that supervisor and supervisee need 'to contact the somatic unconscious' (2008: 90) and develop a sensitivity and capacity for 'very painful states of being to be more fully alive in ourselves and in our patients' (ibid: 100).

That supervisor and supervisee need to do this work together is emphasised by Frizell in her writing entitled *Embodiment and the Supervisory Task* (2012) and by Klapisch-Cohen:

> When one comprehends therapy and supervision as being-in-becoming, one no longer relates only to the individual as separated but rather to the "becoming through the dialogue". The acceptance of both supervisor and supervisee, to share an embodied emotional experience and create an open authentic dialog, enables this meeting to take place.
>
> (2015: 151)

Such authentic dialogue in supervision also needs to include a critical awareness of power relationships observed in the client's life, between client and therapist as well as between supervisor and supervisee. There is always a possibility that one woman might be participating in and embodying systems that violate another woman. Taylor in her reflections on relationship in feminist therapy reminds us and herself 'not only to accompany my clients as they examine the texture and intricate details of their experience, but also to not be naïve to the likelihood that my privilege is underwritten by another's oppression' (2013: 30).

A third mode of holding sacred, articulated in this chapter as the Relishing Body, is the embodied intimacy with self and other through non-directed movement and reciprocal witnessing by supervisor and supervisee. This includes moving with remembered client gestures, movements and bodily states during supervision. As cultivated in the practice of Authentic Movement (Adler, 2002), the witnessing of such non-directed movement does not treat the supervisor's, supervisee's and (imagined) client's bodies 'as objects of analytical scrutiny' (Panhofer et al., 2011: 10). Stromsted elaborates that the witness 'is not *watching* or *observing* the mover, but rather *holding* her in a receptive, compassionate gaze – without interpretation or judgment ...' (2019: 95, italics in original).

Witnessing as a mode of holding sacred also extends to the language that both supervisor and supervisee use to name movement and bodily experience in supervision. It is phenomenological or 'essential' (Stromsted, 2019: 97) in that it describes what is physically seen and strives to differentiate – i.e. 'hold separate' – the various ways in which supervisee, supervisor and clients might internally experience and interpret the physical phenomenon. It is through the modelling and practice of such compassionate gaze and differentiated speaking that supervision can contribute to a field of potential embodiment in which it becomes possible and safe for the client to (re)discover joy and aliveness in and through her body.

Concluding Thoughts

Our collective and creative exploration has brought to paper how we as women hold sacred the woman's body in supervision. In her recollections, reflections and analysis, Sue has illustrated how this can support the woman supervisee in developing and maintaining trust in the fertility of her skills as a therapist. Annette has shown how holding and being held sacred can renew the woman supervisee's capacity to stay present in body when working with women clients who have experienced abuse and violence. Christina has demonstrated that this resources the woman supervisee with body visions of what is possible when working with woman clients towards a greater appetite for life and joy in her own body.

Our writings combined reveal how the quality of our holding sacred is linked to the depth of our relationships grown over time. The process itself of creating, discussing and refining our words on these pages has enriched our relational practice as supervisors and supervisees. The closing act of our research ritual (Figure 9.17) speaks to the core of this practice:

> We take the edges of our collective map, the edges of our body knowledge made visible. We roll them towards each other, inward, to the centre of the map. The further we come the more there is to handle. Our hands are now kneading the body-marked paper, incorporating all materials and words that we have used. It feels like making bread.
>
> Right at the end, there is only one apple left, and one word: to behold. To be and to hold, to be whilst we hold. To be **because** we hold, in our bodies and with our bodies, the seeds and fruit of what **can** be.

Acknowledgements

We would like to thank artist Emma Scott for her beautiful photographs that bring this chapter alive and keep us grounded in its making. We would also like to thank dance movement psychotherapist Hannah Murdoch-Payne who, as a scribe during the ritual, made sure to capture what was fleeting and less visible, thereby greatly adding depth to what is written. Finally, we honour the whole of the collective that has tended to the CBMR over time, thereby laying this chapter's path of enquiry.

Figure 9.17 The closing act: To behold.

References

Adler, J. (2002). *Offering from the Conscious Body*. Vermont: Inner Traditions.

Appleton, M. (2020). *Transitions to Wholeness – Integrating Prenatal, Transpersonal & Somatic Psychology*. Athens: Cosmoanelixis.

Brown, C. (2008). The importance of making art for the creative arts therapist: an artistic inquiry. *The Arts in Psychotherapy*. 35(3): 201–8. DOI: 10.1016/j.aip.2008.04.002

Chodorow, J. (2015). Work in progress – Authentic Movement: Danced and moving active imagination. *Journal of Dance & Somatic Practices*, 7(2): 257–72. DOI: 10.1386/jdsp.7.2.257_1

Curtis, S. (2015). *Woman of Earth*. Retrieved January 18, 2021, from www.annetteschwalbe.co.uk/2015/07/seasons-of-a-woman-july-body-map/

Davis, J. (Ed.) (2000). Ritual as therapy, therapy as ritual. *Journal of Feminist Family Therapy*, 11(4): 115–30. DOI: 10.1300/J086v11n04_09

Frizell, C. (2012). Embodiment and the supervisory task: the supervision of dance movement psychotherapists in training. *Body, Movement and Dance in Psychotherapy*. 7(4): 293–304. DOI: 10.1080/17432979.2012.681394

Frizell, C. (2020, November 10). *This Is the Research; We Are in it. Diffractive Analysis and Post-Qualitative Entanglements of Matter and Matters that Matter* [Lunchtime Talk notes]. London: Goldsmiths College.

Hayes, J. (2013). *Soul and Spirit in Dance Movement Psychotherapy: A Transpersonal Approach.* London: Jessica Kingsley.

Irigaray, L. (1985). *This Sex Which Is Not One*. New York: Cornell University Press.

Jung, C.G. (1968). *The Archetypes and the Collective Unconscious.* (2nd edn). London: Routledge.

Klapisch-Cohen, O. (2015). A cloud and a box: an embodied triangle of imagery work in relational body PTSD psychotherapy supervision. *Body, Movement and Dance in Psychotherapy.* 10(3): 144–52. DOI: 10.1080/17432979.2015.1047406

McNiff, S. (2008). Art-based research. In Knowles, J.G. & Cole, A.L. (Eds.). *Handbook of the Arts in Qualitative Research: Perspective, Methodologies, Examples and Issues.* London: Sage Publications. 29–41.

Menzam-Sills, C. (2020). Out of the dark: embodying our original embryological potential. *Journal of Prenatal and Perinatal Psychology and Health.* 34(6): 443–56.

Panhofer, H., Payne, H., Meekums B. & Parker T. (2011). Dancing, moving and writing in clinical supervision? Employing embodied practices in psychotherapy supervision. *The Arts in Psychotherapy.* 38(1): 9–16. DOI: 10.1016/j.aip.2010.10.001

Parvin, R. (1997). Exploring intimacy in therapy. *Women & Therapy.* 20(1): 69–71. DOI: 10.1300/J015v20n01_11

Ramos, M.N. (2018). Dance/movement therapy and shamanic healing ritual: natural intelligence of body and spirit. *Body, Movement and Dance in Psychotherapy.* 13(1): 50–62. DOI: 10.1080/17432979.2017.1421586

Schwalbe, A., Greenland, C., Curtis, S., & Best, P.A. (2017a). Collective body mapping ritual. *Art Therapy OnLine.* 8(1): 1–21. DOI: 10.25602/GOLD.atol.v8i1.425

Schwalbe, A. (2017b). Understanding the collective body: A body mapping ritual. In Bender, S. (Ed.). *Beyond Frontiers: Movement Analysis and Related Fields,* Berlin: Logos Verlag. 117–29.

Schwalbe, A. (2019). Somatic body mapping with women during times of transition. In Payne, H., Koch, S., Tania, J. & Fuchs, T. (Eds.). *The Routledge International Handbook of Embodied Perspectives in Psychotherapy.* Oxon: Routledge. 104–16.

Stromsted, T. (2014). The alchemy of Authentic Movement: Awakening spirit in the body. In Williamson, A., Whately, S., Batson, G., & Weber R. (Eds.). *Dance, somatics and spiritualities: Contemporary sacred narratives.* Bristol: Intellect Books. 35–60.

Stromsted, T. (2019). Witnessing practice – in the eyes of the beholder. In Payne, H., Koch, S., Tania, J. & Fuchs, T. (Eds.), *The Routledge International Handbook of Embodied Perspectives in Psychotherapy.* Oxon: Routledge. 95–103.

Taylor, S. (2013). Acts of remembering: relationship in feminist therapy. *Women & Therapy,* 36(1–2): 23–34. DOI: 10.1080/02703149.2012.720498

The Holy Bible (1966). Revised Standard Version, Catholic Edition. Hong Kong: Dai Nippon Printing.

Wood, G.W. (2018). *The Psychology of Gender.* London: Routledge.

Woodman, M. (2008). Honouring the body. *Counselling Psychology Quarterly,* 21(2): 119–21. DOI: 10.1080/09515070802066821

Wyman-McGinty, W. (2008). The contribution of Authentic Movement in supervising dance movement therapists. In Payne, H. (Ed.). *Supervision of Dance Movement Psychotherapy,* London: Routledge. 89–102.

Chapter 10

Supervision or Co-vision?

Co-activating a Receptive and Responsive Container for Reflection and Restoration

Katy Dymoke

In my dance movement psychotherapy (DMP) practice, I have experienced supervision in different clinical contexts and I have supervised a wide range of health and somatic practitioners, psychotherapists included. As a large proportion of my practice is with children, vulnerable adults, learning disabled and others lacking capacity, I rely on non-verbal communication and an integrative, ontogenetic perspective from Body-Mind Centering®.[1] Accordingly, I bring the languages of movement and touch to the supervisory process, since these senses are primary to human relationships (Autton, 1989; Bainbridge Cohen, 2012, 2019) and to the praxis of DMP and body-oriented psychotherapies. In my experience as a supervisor, I have found that working with movement effectively bridges the supervisee and therapist selves by tapping into the personal unconscious or pre-conscious self as well as aspects of the professional self. Affective as it is, this predominantly non-verbal realm underlies and enriches the supervisory alliance and informs our reciprocal, reflexive process.

In my experience of embodied supervision, there is a shift in the relational status of supervisee and supervisor when the supervisee enters an explorative, experiential process. In this primarily non-verbal territory, the supervisor may witness from the edge or move with or use touch, as required by the process. The resonant relationship occupies a realm that is contained by a *mutual* deep respect for what the body reveals, for the bodily sense (Gendlin, 1999) and for insights that emerge reflexively during and following this process. It appears that the value of supervision is enhanced by what I perceive in these moments as a co-visory relationship; as I come to explain in the following chapter section where I consider the membrane concept, the relationship has opened from a focused meeting of minds to a corporeal realm, more usual to the therapeutic process. I consider the possibility to move between these realms as essential to the process, for the supervisee to engage with emotional states and associated feelings that arise from the practice or professional context. In moving the questions within this relational sphere, answers arise from the ensuing dialogue and both gain insights into the personal, professional and intrapersonal relationship. This corporeal relational realm is familiar to

DOI: 10.4324/9781003034940-11

the therapeutic process and so to supervision, particularly when in person, in the same room, with the possibility to move and touch.[2]

Through examples taken from my practice, I seek to reiterate and elucidate the value of the corporeal as the resource for managing the complexities of human relationships, finding answers to questions that bewilder the mind and releasing old patterns or beliefs that reside bodily and manifest as restrictions or conflict. Essentially, an embodied approach to supervision enables a reciprocal exchange through movement and the languaging of aspects that remain untouched and veiled in the explicitly verbal relationship. Inevitably I question the restrictive semantic implications of the term 'super-visor' for the witness who is available bodily, and more appropriately as 'co-visor', to use the resource of her lived (embodied) experience. Each vignette is a composite case; I have made alterations to retain confidentiality and conversations are recreated from knowing the person, to recapture our relational dynamic, they are not verbatim quotations.

The Membrane Concept – the Safe Container for Embodied Supervision

In this context, the membrane concept is a depersonalised hermeneutic for the mutable and permeable container of the co-visory relationship the realm in which the supervisory subject or content is re-experienced and explored. Movement is inherent to the DMP process, likewise to the co-visioning process – it is used to attend to the phenomenality of the body in the psychotherapeutic process, to unveil and explore the complex multiplicity of roles and responsibilities therein (Meekums, 2002, 2006; Totton, 2015). The membrane stems from being aware of the limitations of what we may hold dear, and how permeable we are to the influence of historical hierarchies or sociological constructs (Varela et al., 1999; Depraz, 2003; Marosan, 2009) such as touch taboo – which have also been pertinently described as 'veils of perception' (Harre & Gillet, 1994: 42).

The Plasma Membrane – From Cell to Cellular Consciousness – The Body–Mind Continuum

I initially encountered the anatomy of a human cell membrane through embodied practice as a student of Body-Mind Centering® (BMC®) in 1992. The membrane is familiar to many, at the experiential level of the skin, or the tissues underlying. Each human cell is contained and bodily defined by its bilipid membrane; two layers of fatty molecules enable motility, and the thousands of protein channels and receptors enable permeability, intra- and inter-cellular communication and homoeostasis. A cell membrane establishes the tactile 'animate form' (Sheets-Johnstone, 1990: 301) of the cell body, supporting regulation and sustaining inner stasis, and manifests this outwardly as bodily sense or 'cellular consciousness' – a state that Bainbridge Cohen differentiates from 'brain' consciousness in the embodiment process (Bainbridge Cohen, 2012: 157). In embodying my self-membrane, by touching and moving with it, I sensed and felt that it contained me, and enabled communication between my mind and my bodily self. From within the inner facing layer, I encountered a corporeal sense of self – of my body image (Schilder, 1970) – and expressed this outwardly to others from the outer layer. Fundamentally the two layers shaped my identity, in terms of what I had learned and chosen to reveal, retain or deny.

The membrane is where aspects or attributes that I may have received from others, reside. Some I may veil, or keep hidden within and may need to dispel (Butler, 2005; Noe, 2009). Self-embodiment is key for the membrane to serve the communication and self-regulatory needs that underlie self-other relationships. As we all have cells with membranes, this commonality enables relational attunement, empathy and support, and a context in which the subjective self can be transcendent, in which new perceptions are admitted and their value made evident – as in embodied co-vision.

Some Features of the Membrane Concept – in Supervision

With both an inner and an outer surface, the membrane may be used metaphorically as a means to analyse relational dynamics between diverse identities or selves. As a fluid structure, the membrane presents reflexive potential for re-patterning, it may also restrain or separate. A part of the animate self, the *motile* membrane is receptive and responsive to inner and outer states of awareness. *Permeability* enables release of fixed or restricted patterns that can inhibit new ways of being and restrain change, it provides space for modulation, alignment and balance. *Mutability* tests the membrane's resilience to the unknown and provides the ability to change without fear of losing the self. *Non-permeability* may cause stress, conflict, anxiety or confusion, inhibiting motility; impeding movement and manifestation of other aspects of the self that could be beneficial to know.

As a container for the supervisory process, the membrane initially occupies the *space* between the practitioners, providing a domain for exchange. The membrane is a relational necessity, like a boundary, but like living tissue it has an inherent permeability to permit learning, healing and maturation (Martz and Lindy, 2010). The co-visory membrane is a locus of, and for, movement of mind; a place for recognition, retrospection, co-witnessing and co-discovery, with the benefit of 'hindsight': it creates a space–time continuum in which to clarify, regulate and disentangle the psychotherapeutic process – another continuum.

Unlike a boundary, a membrane is not fixed or singular, there may be layers or enfolded membranes where sense-data transitions in, or out, manifesting the imprints of past experience or societal diktat influencing choice. These membranes create a perceptive realm where new patterns of thinking take shape, where the values of diversity and inclusivity inherent to DMP, provide the philosophical 'glue' to ensure an ethic of care. In the examples I consider below, the membrane is animate, and encompasses the process of apperception – of actively assimilating aspects of a new experience within a 'body' of existing knowledge.

The Three Membranes

The following vignettes indicate how these attributes are relevant to embodied supervision. In some cases, working with movement sets thinking aside and creates space to attend to the 'self-giveness' of the experience, to the attributes that evade words and 'self-evidence' of the psychotherapist self (Marosan, 2009: 78). The first, self-membrane, is an intra-subjective realm for the supervisee and supervisor to each have a discrete immersive space that is permeable to being seen and heard, sensed and felt, by the other. A supervisee usually requires time to pay attention to her own experience (within her self-membrane), with the supervisor (attuned and attentive in her self-membrane) providing discrete empathic support. The second, intersubjective membrane becomes a familiar and mutual space-time realm between them, where a movement-based dialogical process is defined by their roles. If a third subject, such as the client, colleague, or other supervisory subjects, is presented, a third membrane is admitted into the second membrane as a movement metaphor or a more discursive form. Potential for change can then emerge from the reflexive interpersonal exchange, to impact on the client or wider society, whether in some transcendental or more pragmatic way. The three membranes provide an animate space for the client to be held and ensure the supervisee's duty of care to the client remains ethically reflexive (Etherington, 2007).

In my experience (and as I seek to unpack in the vignettes), at the point where the supervisor steps in to support or facilitate, particularly when the personal and professional selves collide or resonate, this may enable further transparency or an unveiling of the complexity of roles. As a somatically engaged supervisor, I wish to share how I sense and feel these self-aspects manifest, and how their attributes resolve or regulate satisfactorily through our reflexive exchange. This status has sustained a sense of trust. By 'hand holding' the supervisee's personal self, I support their professional self to explore and follow the challenging paths, events and attributes brought by the client and the responses that shape the therapeutic alliance. Somatically, the permeable membrane grounds a fluid dialogical relationship that enables these multiple identities to overlap, to effectively 'speak' to each other and develop professionally, forthwith.

Vignette 1. The Three Membranes

I start with an example taken from journal notes following a session with my DMP supervisor that involved movement and interpersonal touch. The session revealed to me how effectively a safe and embodied supervisory alliance provides a reciprocally held and entrusting space, one in which 'truth' may appear and vulnerability be transformed, instilling self-trust whilst facilitating self-reflection. The three membranes (self, combined and supervisory subject), manifest within an interpersonal and dialogical alliance, I number them 1–3 as they appear, and reference them in the notes that follow. Together within a relational continuum (membrane 2) the supervisory subject is processed and my personal and professional selves find coherence. The event takes about 35 minutes.

> *Feeling I can collapse and cry and move through the images*
> *deeply held emotion, anger, shame*
> *Being held as a supervisee (point 1 below)*
> *Appreciation. Showing appreciation.*
> *Feeling wisdom – in the holding.*
> *Feeling wisdom in the listening.*
> *Feeling myself open (point 2 below)*
> *Feeling myself fall*
> *Crumble,*
> *Want to wail into the void (point 3 below)*
> *Wanting to pull at institutional injustice and tear it with my teeth*
> *I wail, I feel unsafe, I curl into a ball, and she holds me then.*
> *From that root I find light*

I note the membranes:

1   The process of self-immersion in the 'images' that I embody in movement established the first membrane and here I recognise the presence of the supervisor in her membrane and indicate the second membrane of the shared supervisory landscape.
2   Movement underlies the words and process.
3   The bodily sense finds regulation in expression – the inner shards of past experience surface to be seen and heard and can be released back into the inner void safely, as I am held, anchored, and from there the issue is processed.

This meeting takes place in the second membrane which creates a 'buffer zone' where my co-visor shields me from further trauma (Martz and Lindy, 2010). I re-find myself and am figuratively 'reborn' as expressed in the last sentence; 'From that root I find light'. This introspective self-reflective account captures layers of emotions and corporeal responses to externally imposed threats (Vermersch, 1999). Held by the solace, empathy and unconditional support, my inner voices are heard, I am seen, held and connect in movement, sound and physical contact. The roles of psychotherapist, supervisee and supervisor overlap with awareness of the contingency of this moment to the restoration of my personal and professional self-identities.

Meeting the need of the supervisee can, as in this case, resemble meeting a client's need in a two-person therapy model and lies at the heart of the work. This example indicates the type of wisdom and holding that embodied supervision offers; it is a means to unveil undisclosed bodily affect imprints and to assimilate latent patterns or responses safely away from their place of practice. In the above instance, in which I received the support I needed to restore self-belief, my professional self could continue to heal. Succinctly put, there are permeable membranes between the personal and professional selves; my supervisor responded to a silent invitation to step in; in touching me our self-membranes merged at the level of the skin. The ethical value of touch is transparent and clear in this landscape – it is a safe membranous connection for transmission and healing, not a boundary violation (Dymoke, 2014).

Underlying this process is an inherent and implicit understanding based on trust in the bodily sense that arises in a transparent and clear manner, or equally, from the shards of experience that emerge unbridled as a somatic transference or as an emotively resistant counter-transference (Maroda, 1999). As my journal extract evokes, the membranous realm is animate, dialogical, substantial and effective. The relationship is built on trust in the process, which may be empathic or conflictive but always within a continuum that is non-authoritarian and non-hierarchical, in which denial and restraint are circumvented by respect for the potential for change. This co-created embodied realm offers unconditional regard for the constraints or complexes that may otherwise impact on the therapeutic alliance, and so the client. In the following vignettes, the membrane construct underpins the supervisory alliance in order to admit the inherent corporeal, preconscious elements of an intrapersonal dilemma, safely within an interpersonal continuum – an entrusted space for growth.

Vignette 2. The Motile Membrane

In this vignette, I recognise the educational role of the supervisor to support the supervisee to manage the client who, through choice and social immobility, struggles to identify the constraints that impede or influence the choices he makes. It requires motility of mind, to open to new potential rather than close in on its lack. The self-membrane in this example of co-vision appears intra-personally self-regulatory, the second, reflexively interpersonal.

The supervisee grapples with a projection of vulnerability and inadequacy. Her professional self is experiencing a projective identification from her manager *that DMP is ineffective – which she described as; 'I want to be valued by my client **and** to show my manager how valuable this work is'. This internalised idea of her inadequate professional self is partially due to being a recent graduate seeking to prove her worth to a manager who measures her success primarily by case load output. The issue she brings to supervision is that a male client has chosen to interrupt the therapy to try counselling. She is conflicted; she takes it personally but also sees an opportunity to close a problematic client case. Her manager projects that DMP is less appropriate for a man, which conflicts with her values and undermines her DMP self-identity.*

I invite an opportunity to move, to process and explore her confusion. After some fragmented movement she makes broad open arm movements as if pushing it all behind her. I see her find her kinesphere and reinstate her 'self-membrane' by becoming immersed in her movement. She has a strong centre and starts to connect to her limbs sweeping outwards to the periphery. Her familiar mover-self finds an anchor in being witnessed and the co-articulation we engage in reaffirms her DMP identity. In this spacious context she regains a sense of integrity and can set her personal issues aside; she accepts to close the case with regard to his demands and recognises his inability to self-regulate and to commit to a process he isn't ready for. In contemplating the manager issue we agree that she writes a case closure report in which she outlines the benefits of the intervention and how they were met using DMP.

Some weeks later after short term therapy, the client requests recommencing. The manager is wary of indulging him. His clinical needs are discussed again at pre-assessment; he reiterates the value of movement methods for self-regulation and self-worth. In supervision the supervisee considers whether to take him back on and agrees to move this question. Unsettled and defensive, her movement is erratic and ungrounded, she is activated and appears reluctant to engage with herself. I sense a transference of a protest response, in her raised voice, implying a lack of containment. I witness the impact of her manager's projective identification in conflict with the desire to prove her worth, it impedes the process to make a decision.

From my membrane I return to the client, why refuse his request? How does this position manifest bodily? Her movement slows down and she listens. I had intuited a need to explore the spoken assumptions about the client, to then set them aside and notice what else is present – in a quieter, non-verbal realm, a place to regulate her anxiety through movement. Our shared membrane became a safe place to admit and explore her veiled self, non-verbally. I witnessed and held the space, listening and mirroring back the 'professional' reflexive DMP, noticing an increase in coherence arise. After a pause, I asked her if she felt able to address the client now; 'Yes I realise this is what he needs – a trustful person to hold a space for him to experience his ability to believe in himself more, to meet those who doubt his capacity.' I witness her clarity, she witnesses how strong her body feels, and asserts she can accompany him; she could now allow for the complexity he presented to clarify her task. He depended on her to step up and step into his world to sense and feel the impact of the injustice he experienced as a man disabled by society. I inquired if he appeared as demanding now. She realised how hard he was fighting for justice and how exhausting it must be to fight, to be who you are, all the time. She saw a parallel with her own fight to prove her worth to herself.

In this session, self-movement is a reflexive modality, an effective way to separate from the projective identification of the inadequate professional and the judgement it instilled. She integrated the incoherent movement that had been its expression, resolving the underlying conflict through self-dialog. A clear self-membrane returned as her selves conversed in movement and were seen in my witnessing. Our shared understanding of the value of DMP enabled her to restore a positive self-perception. She found clarity first for herself, and then as the professional engagement with the client, she was able to dispose of her manager's projections and affirmed, for herself, the value of DMP. Within the realm of movement, and verbal exchange, all three supervisory subjects benefitted, as did DMP as a profession. The three membranes showed us the options and the pathway for decision-taking – reflexively, fluidly and impartially.

Vignette 3. The Permeable Membrane in Co-vision – An Embodied Transpersonal Space

In this third vignette, I introduce a further fluid aspect of the membrane. Informed by BMC developmental movement and touch-based approaches, the transitional 'mind' of the membrane is inherent in its permeable and tactile receptive structure. As in this case, its role as a receptive and responsive container becomes apparent in its reflexive and restorative role in self-regulation and as a locus for the reunification of psyche with soma (Hayes, 2013). The image of the membrane depicts the fluid transition between states of consciousness, a continuum of spiritual and earthly life that reunites psyche as soul and spirit, resonant, transcendent and body. In this case, the membrane is used with mindful intention, to perceive the 'molecules' and particles of sense that the visual sense fails to access but which movement is akin to (Gibson, 1966). In this instance the second membrane concept is informed by the trauma membrane concept of Martz and Lindy (2010); in which the 'buffer zone' provides a protective shield against further traumatic events, for the trauma to heal, at a time when it may still be unavailable to others (Martz and Lindy, 2010:27).

A supervisee arrives, she has lost a close family member. Although on compassionate leave, 'supervision' is still a requirement as her grief impacts on her return to work and is a professional issue. The ache of loss is tangible, the tendency for stillness an indication of psyche being in flight, as if to accompany the departing soul of the relative. In this situation her self-membrane is fluid, and unstable, and client work a challenge – she needs containment and support not the weight of responsibility at this time. I review this moment from the lens of the mutual membrane that took form between us, from the resonant contact of each other's deep sense of the pain and its intangible yet tsunami like impact on every cell of the body. As a permeable form in the void, our co-created membrane is where psyche restores its bodily form and finds comfort, and stability. This co-visory realm is transcendental, a place for solace, assimilation and release – a necessary process before being able to resume clinical work.

We sit facing each other, sat on the floor in a studio. We chose to be in this space for this session, anticipating the opportunity to move or if not to have the possibility for it. I recall feeling porous, still, monochrome and quiet.

I feel her sorrow, there is a softness in the membrane – the softness of being bereft, the potential to dissolve, to collapse. After some moments of resonance, there is a shift in state. As we move particles of affect release with this outflow, transcending the void with images that form from the fragments, distilled from the flux between us, the ache of nostalgia shared, it feels as if the direction of the emotional tide brings clarity, and her breath and voice bring warmth and colour. A change occurs, captured in an image I don't recall whose;

A bird will fly from the nest...

Arising; movement and mindful reflection fill the space of loss and hope for healing conflicts with concern for the pain. I lean into my self-membrane to avoid being drawn into confusion, feeling the latent irrationality of trying to make sense of this in words. This landscape is familiar to my therapist self, as when I absorb and filter from what is present in order to find an essence, or suspend all thinking to allow more substance to emerge and inform. My previous personal loss of my father arises there. I consider now how I presented it to her and how it moved us. His presence illuminates my mind, awash with warm light. I share that "he hasn't left, my father is still here". Some of it will have a resonance with her, creating some sense of solidity, and in chiming we affirm the sense of loss, like the bird it can then take flight – made tangible, perceptible, acceptable, separate.

I brought this focus, the sense of what follows, to evoke an eventual return to stasis, to self. The membrane felt restored by reference to a reality from past experience, I witnessed it appear and encompass both like an embrace – much needed, intuitively and reciprocally formed. This response felt indicative of the therapeutic alliance in which empathic resonance and strong countertransference can overwhelm the membrane. If too permeable the role of the membrane is lost and the flux can overwhelm and tear it apart. Knowing the membrane as an animate space in which affect can flow, gently and in its own time, I am at the juncture of the supervisor – therapist roles; I assume the therapeutic responsibility of the supervisor to modulate, to pause, to invite release by inviting the waves of affect to lap against the membrane, rather than imbue it. Such moments leave space within the respective self-membranes for bodily sense to restore its substance, which then permeates a sense of stasis and stability. The first membrane is sustained by shared lived experience and glimpses of a future beyond the here and now, offering light and understanding, to calm or stem the flow. The supervisee is then able to return to her therapist role.

The supervisee needed courage to bring her loss to supervision. Expecting to be met somatically, her wish was to find support, compassion and acceptance. With our attuned, mutual lightness, our shared bodily sense affirmed the bond between us and our robust shared membrane. Our personal and professional selves, now removed from their respective environments, find stasis within this co-created realm and entrusted roles. Deep listening creates space for the potential to arise (signified by the bird?); the emotional outflow mediates and alleviates the pain; the inflow of solace, recovery and rest gives space for acceptance of endings and new beginnings. Now with greater resilience, she feels able to move with the support of her own membrane to keep separate her personal from her professional life.

In my experience, embodied supervision is contingent on an evolved relationship; to let go of fear or loss requires comfort and holding, like the symbiotic realms of intercellular communication between mother and infant, in which the encompassing interdependency is natural to the process of ontogenesis and maturation (Montagu, 1986; Bainbridge Cohen, 2012; Ettinger, 2006; Sheets- Johnstone, 1990, 2010). Years of embodied inquiry and experience underlies my trust in the membrane concept, in the process of re-assimilation of fragmented selves. In setting aside the supervisor and supervisee roles, we created space to be available and present, to explore the emotional tide of loss in the context of her practice and to affirm the value of the body in client work.

Vignette 4. The Mutable Membrane

This vignette explores the potential for the supervisor to hold the supervisee's multiple selves from past and present within the alliance. Embodied supervision was new and of interest to this experienced psychotherapist. He worked with families and was curious to explore his professional self through movement and body-oriented methods. On this occasion, he brought a counter-transference in which his child-self appeared whilst attending to an adopted young client and early childhood memories continued to activate him. He had maintained his professional role and stated with some trepidation that exploring the memory together would enable him to safely explore the ingrained attributes of abandonment and neglect. I intuited that his inner child could not be safely referenced until the veiled psycho-emotional effects were available, re-experienced and anchored by renewed sense of coherence and stasis that his self-membrane would discover and embody together with me in mine. Our alliance was based on an agreement that supervision is a place to admit the body as a professional issue, in an experiential process. On this occasion, I use the first and third person to evoke the second (shared) membrane, at work.

We begin sitting and you give an account of your difficulty to move with your child clients. I realise I am moving within, receptive to the ebb and flow of your story, whether in gesture, tone of voice, posture; my being registers sense, awaits a time to contribute. I am familiar with your discomfort with movement and your anticipated moment of movement is immanent. The unspoken personal self is veiled by dread, shame, denial, for fear of 'the worst that could possibly happen'…like the adder in the grass.

You recall being a timid child, seldom accompanied by your parents, this sense has already permeated our membrane and was imprinted in your bodily-sense – you are uncomfortable and unsure as if ashamed of being seen – which you evidently crave but have always been neglected.

I note the unfamiliarity of you being accompanied and seen and say that as your supervisor I do not judge or impose conditions or expectations (other than the usual safeguarding caveat). I listen and notice my inner visceral state, these conscious thoughts and dialog assist our process, stabilise the membrane and enable movement. I ask;

'How do you feel in this moment?'

'Uncertain, shame and sadness.'

'Shall we try to 'move' this, it may shed light on your inhibition to move with your clients?'

'Yes. Good idea.'

'I will witness you and check in with you?'

'Yes good.' You stand up in front of the chair and move – uncomfortable, awkward, eyes down. I respond;

'So I see you move as you feel and attend to that…to where in your body your feelings are located. I see this is difficult and I am here to hold you.'

Your body moves spatially and face downcast…reducing in size so the space appears larger, your bodily-sense reveals a new landscape, a relocation of self in movement, a deforming and reforming of body shape within its self-membrane.

As you move, the inner-you finds his way into the whole body and shame retreats. I sense now that the second membrane, previously between us, widens to contain us – the substance that is condensed in bodily form moves within the space – there is no 'right' word to speak and words are our usual substrate. This space is new for us but familiar to me, evoking trust and safety. Your movement is still within but it starts to surface in perceptible fragments; you step forward and back, wrap your arms around you, hold tightly, then find your way onto a mat on the floor, lying on your back. As you become more receptive to yourself you appear available, receptive to my witnessing.

Now your body is still but emanates discomfort, arching back stiffly, I think, 'support'. I then feel separated from your vulnerability and disengaged, the membrane has changed constellation; it is like a self-exclusion zone, ambiguous and easily misread. You curl into yourself and turn on your side tightly. I feel a void. This moment of separation animates me, challenges me to attend to my senses, my own bodily sense and to reconnect, since abandonment and neglect is our theme. I change my position and sit on the floor, moving gently closer. Now you are still curled up on the floor, on one side, even the slightest vibration of my being felt too loud. My voice came in that space before the thought made itself known...

'Would you like a hand somewhere?' It is a tone I don't recognise, a tone that speaks the unfamiliarity of this moment.

'Yes... on my back, behind my head.'

We reinstate the second membrane, this unanticipated relational field, you vulnerable and alone, but held, as if dropped and abandoned, vulnerable to all kinds of ill intent but safe here. The idea that touching is deviant or taboo is supplanted by your consent, by your need for unconditional support, from myself as supervisor for you to meet yourself fully in this place. Your need for contact comes via your bodily form, transmitted from your membrane to mine. This vibrational field comes from something unveiled after many years of hiding, through a bodily form of a being that is at once old yet desperately young, infantile, who had never been held, fully, for long enough to feel worth, to feel home, to feel 'here I am'.

My hand finds your back, my other hand finds the back of your head. It is like finding a landscape that had been created by the felt sense that needs to be made into substance. I am part of the shaping and for several minutes, a part of the substance. Meaning is not found in my hands, nor in the back of your head, but from the whole space and time, within the membrane. You start to breathe more deeply and thank me. My hands accept and come away. This is the first and last time I touch you, that you were touched by me, that your inner child is accompanied by me.

This is a moment of return, of nostalgia for something missing now found. Sitting up a few feet away we see each other. The landscape is like a mill pond, then I ask;

'How are you?'

You are sitting up on the mat and looking calm, clutching your knees to your chest. 'Yes I wanted to be touched and couldn't ask, thank you.'

I responded; 'I felt asked. I asked because this is new territory.'

For this supervisee, the space to move became a transcendental space in which to meet aspects of self he had shut away. In admitting the desire to experience touch and movement the supervisory alliance provides answers and new insights for him to anchor his practice. Significantly, the authenticity of his foetal-like bodily form indicates safety, and touch indicates trust and a means to hold us in the present. His trauma surfaces from deep within and becomes available to re-experience in an embodied, and essentially co-visory realm, where meeting his child self and aligning with him is contingent on the intimacy and proximity of our shared membrane. An adopted young client, who is absent, comes to my mind, evoking the third membrane that we hold together and the space to embrace them.

Regardless of my specialist touch training and research in BMC and psychotherapy, touch is unfamiliar to supervision and implies therapeutic intervention rather than a supervisory objective. Why is this raised here if the unfamiliarity of touch and movement disappears with the membrane concept? In the context of embodied supervision, touch and movement practices enable a co-visory process which, essentially, provides a space to explore and to learn to use touch with clients for whom it is the right language, even if only once. I think of those who have been touch deprived historically and currently in the pandemic. Touch allows their story to be heard and exists as an active part of embodied psychotherapeutic practice, no longer obfuscated by societal non-touch diktat or denied; touch is admissible in the membrane where it is innately inextricable from movement (Bainbridge Cohen, 2012; Dymoke, 2019, 2021).

Inevitably, this supervisory alliance evolved according to what the supervisee sought to explore and on the co-visory model on offer: its territory, philosophy and landscape. This process does not replace personal therapy, it addresses the internal conflicts initiated directly by a client case and professional context or indirectly as a representation of something more general, like institutional injustice, that permeates from beyond the room.

I witnessed the supervisee experience the possibility to let go of a pre-existing self-identity that prevented him from opening to a new pathway or self-reconstruct. Embodied supervision is a purposeful place for someone who dislikes ultimatums and preordained truths, and serves those who prefer to listen and hold the possibility that the social landscape is co-determined. In co-vision, a shared epistemology evolves to evidence the phenomena that appear to consciousness as self-evident, demonstrable, if existential, truths (Marosan, 2009).

In these four vignettes, the membrane concept has served the supervisory alliance. It has established an intimate and ethically situated environment in which complexities can be admitted and explored, in which professional issues that appear directive towards rules and regulations can be addressed experientially. This interpersonal level of inquiry provides a place for mutual learning of benefit to the psychotherapeutic endeavour. It is not a guarantee of correction, it is a reflexive animate space in which questions are not necessarily pre-empted but possible answers are excavated that reposition the initial projection or retention as the question. The client, supervisee and supervisor participate in redefining 'clinical supervision' as an embodied practice.

Being a supervisor implies an objective advisory role that may involve bridging a gap between the supervisee's personal and professional selves, or revisiting the roots of current beliefs and conflicts taking place between these selves or within the therapeutic alliance. The assumed non-authoritative status of the supervisor does not neglect these ethical responsibilities or deny an advisory, consultative and valuable epistemology; such humility permits the supervisee her own 'authority' over her sensed experience. Once registered bodily and then known perceptually, it becomes epistemic, affirming the progression from non-verbal communication to dialogue and mutual understanding.

The roots of this relational realm are available if we are receptive and pragmatic about the bodily sense, the unitary being and the plausibility of self-reconstruction (Sheets-Johnstone, 1990, Bainbridge Cohen, 2012). I recognise the regulatory role of the supervisor to indicate how personal and professional beliefs impede the process of identifying the client's need; facilitating disclosure; and engaging in the healing process to find the 'therapeutic elements' such as touch and movement, to heal the 'tear in the tissue of the holistic self' (Martz and Lindy, 2010: 28). The membrane concept contains and enables my dialogue with the supervisee, to find pathways back and forth from the preconscious to the conscious, where we discover the value of embodied supervision.

Notes

1 BMC® and Body-Mind Centering® are registered service marks of Bonnie Bainbridge Cohen, used with permission.
2 I acknowledge the pandemic situation in which online supervision has impacted on proximity and touch.

References

Autton, N. (1989). *Touch, An Exploration.* London: Darton Longman and Todd.
Bainbridge Cohen, B. (2012). *Sensing Feeling and Action. The Experiential Anatomy of Body-Mind Centering®.* (3rd edn). Northampton MA: Contact Editions.
Bainbridge Cohen, B. (2019). *Basic Neurocellular Patterns.* El Sobrante: Burchfield Rose.
Butler, J. (2005). *Giving and Account of Oneself.* New York: Fordham University Press.
Depraz, N. Varela, F.J. & Vermersch, P. (2003). *On Becoming Aware; A pragmatics of Experiencing.* Amsterdam: John Benjamins.
Dymoke, K. (2014). Contact improvisation, the non-eroticized touch in an 'art-sport', *Journal of Dance and Somatic Practice* 6(2): 205–18, DOI: 10.1386/jdsp.6.2.205_1
Dymoke, K. (2017). The Lost and Found. In S. Daniel & C. Trevarthen (Eds.) *Rhythms of Relating in Children's Therapies.* London: Jessica Kingsley. 172-87.
Dymoke, K. (2019) . Touching the Untouchables. *International Journal of Politics and Psychotherapy.* 17(3) DOI: 10.1002/1506
Dymoke, K. (2021). *The Impact of Touch in Dance Movement Psychotherapy; A Body-Mind Centering Approach.* Bristol: Intellect.
Etherington, K. (2007). Ethical Research in Reflexive Relationships. *Qualitative Inquiry,* 13: 599–616. DOI: 10.1177/1077800407301175
Ettinger, B. L. (2006). *The Matrixial Borderspace.* Minnesota: University of Minnesota Press.

Gibson, J. J (1966). *The Senses Considered as Perceptual Systems*. Boston: Houghton Mifflin.

Gendlin, E. T. (1999) A New Model. In F. Varela & J. Shear (Eds.) *The View from Within. First-Person Approaches to the study of consciousness*. Thorverton: Imprint Academic. 232–237.

Harre, R., & Gillett, G. (1994). *The Discursive Mind*. Thousand Oaks & London: Sage.

Hayes, J. (2013). *Soul and Spirit in Dance Movement Psychotherapy A Transpersonal Approach*. London: Jessica Kingsley.

Maroda, K. J. (1999). *Seduction, Surrender, and Transformation: Emotional Engagement in the Analytic Process*. Hillsdale: Analytic Press.

Marosan, B. (2009). Apodicity and Transcendental Phenomenology. *Perspectives: International Postgraduate Journal of Philosophy* 2 (1):78–101.

Martz, E. & Lindy, J. (2010). Exploring the Trauma Membrane Concept. In Springer (Ed.) *Trauma Rehabilitation after War and Conflict* [Online]. Munich: Springer Science & Business Media. http://media.axon.es/pdf/85137_2.pdf

Meekums, B. (2002). *Dance Movement Psychotherapy, A Creative Psychotherapeutic Approach*. London: Sage.

Meekums, B. (2006). Embodiment in dance movement therapy training and practice. In H. Payne (Ed.) *Dance Movement Therapy: Theory, Research and Practice*. (2nd edn.) London: Routledge. 167–83.

Montagu, A. (1986). *Touching: The Human Significance of the Skin*. London: Harper and Row.

Noe, A. (2009). *Out of Our Heads; Why You Are Not Your Brain and Other Lessons from the Biology of Consciousness*. New York: Hill and Wang.

Schilder, P. (1970). *The Image and Appearance of the Human Body; Studies in Constructive Energies of the Psyche*. New York: International Universities Press.

Sheets-Johnstone, M. (1990). *The Roots of Thinking*. Philadelphia: Temple University Press.

Sheets-Johnstone, M. (2010). Kinesthetic experience; understanding movement inside and out. *Body Movement and Dance in Psychotherapy*. 5(2): 111–27. DOI:10.1080/17432979.2010.496221

Tortora, G.J. & Grabowski, S.R. (2000). *Principles of Anatomy and Physiology*. New York: Wiley.

Totton, N. (2015). *Embodied Relating; The Ground of Psychotherapy*. London: Karnac Books.

Varela, F.J. & Shear, J. (1999). First Person Methodologies: What, Why, How? *Journal of Consciousness Studies,* 6(2–3): 1–14.

Vermersch, P. (1999). Introspection as practice. In J. Shear & F.J. Varela (Eds.) *First Person Approaches to the Study of Consciousness*. Thorverton: Imprint Academic. 17-42.

Index

For Product Safety Concerns and Information please contact our EU
representative GPSR@taylorandfrancis.com
Taylor & Francis Verlag GmbH, Kaufingerstraße 24, 80331 München, Germany

www.ingramcontent.com/pod-product-compliance
Ingram Content Group UK Ltd.
Pitfield, Milton Keynes, MK11 3LW, UK
UKHW021455080625
459435UK00012B/507